Bahamas

Robert Barlas and Yong Jui Lin

Marshall Cavendish
Benchmark
New York

PICTURE CREDITS

Cover: © Greg Johnston/Danita Delimont

alt.type/Reuters: 67 • Art Directors/Trip: 49, 51 • Audrius Tomonis: 135 • Bes Stock: 29, 32, 50, 91, 99, 114, 116, 117, 118, 121, 129 • Corbis: 13, 26, 44, 59, 63, 65, 68, 73, 74, 81, 90, 92, 96, 112, 115 • Dave G. Houser: 55 • David Simson: 76, 86, 95, 126 • Focus Team—Italy: 16, 119, 128 • Francis Tan: 130, 131 • Getty Images: 5, 35, 39, 41, 42, 45, 46, 62, 77, 79, 82, 84, 85, 89, 102, 103, 111, 120 • International Photobank: 40 • Jason Laure: 127 • Lonely Planet Images: 9, 33, 71, 94, 122 • North Wind Pictures Archives: 30 • photolibrary: 1, 3, 6, 8, 10, 11, 12, 14, 15, 17, 19, 20, 22, 24, 31, 38, 43, 47, 48, 52, 53, 54, 56, 57, 58, 60, 61, 64, 66, 69, 70, 72, 75, 78, 80, 83, 93, 98, 100, 101, 104, 105, 106, 107, 108, 109, 113, 124 • Topfoto: 25, 27, 28, 36

PRECEDING PAGE

Locals and tourists enjoying the beautiful beach in Nassau, New Providence.

Publisher (U.S.): Michelle Bisson
Editors: Deborah Grahame, Mindy Pang
Copyreader: Sherry Chiger
Designers: Nancy Sabato, Benson Tan
Cover picture researcher: Connie Gardner
Picture researcher: Thomas Khoo

Marshall Cavendish Benchmark
99 White Plains Road
Tarrytown, NY 10591
Website: www.marshallcavendish.us

Originated and designed by Times Media Private Limited
An imprint of Marshall Cavendish International (Asia) Private Limited
A member of Times Publishing Limited

Marshall Cavendish is a trademark of Times Publishing Limited.

All Internet sites were correct and accurate at the time of printing. All monetary figures in this publication are in U.S. dollars.

Library of Congress Cataloging-in-Publication Data
Barlas, Robert.
    Bahamas / Robert Barlas & Yong Jui Lin. — [2nd ed.].
        p. cm. — (Cultures of the world)
    Includes bibliographical references and index.
    Summary: "Provides comprehensive information on the geography, history,
        wildlife, governmental structure, economy, cultural diversity, peoples,
        religion, and culture of the Bahamas" — Provided by publisher.
    ISBN 978-1-60870-021-9
    1. Bahamas—Juvenile literature. I. Yong, Jui Lin. II. Title.
    F1651.2.B37 2010
    972.96—dc22   2010000729

Printed in China
7 6 5 4 3 2 1

CONTENTS

090

INTRODUCTION

THE COMMONWEALTH OF THE BAHAMAS consists of about 2,700 islands and cays , nearly 2,000 of which are little more than rock formations jutting above sea level. This single country is spread out over 90,000 square miles (233,100 square km) of the Atlantic Ocean, off the southwestern coast of Florida. Most people know the Bahamas as a popular tourist destination, famous for its vast sandy beaches and opportunities to snorkel and scuba-dive. These idyllic tropical islands have a colorful history: They have been a pirates' kingdom and part of the vast British Empire, and today they are an independent country with a democratically elected government. Over the centuries the Bahamas also acquired its migrant population, with the result that its people are as diverse as its history. The Bahamas is still in many ways a tropical paradise for its citizens and for tourists, but new challenges are emerging. As global warming worsens, natural disasters such as hurricanes are affecting the Bahamas more often. The global economic slowdown has meant that tourist arrivals have dropped, having an adverse effect on the Bahamian economy and employment. The Bahamians, with their characteristic optimism, are looking to a future full of potential still to be realized.

GEOGRAPHY

A view of the clear turquoise water and tidal estuary surrounding the islands of the Bahamas.

THE BAHAMAS IS AN ARCHIPELAGO lying in the Atlantic Ocean off the coast of Florida. South of the Bahamas are Cuba, Haiti, and the Dominican Republic, while southeast are the Turks and Caicos Islands. The Tropic of Cancer runs through the middle of the Bahamas.

Exactly how many islands there are in the Bahamas depends on whether one counts every cay, even the ones that are no more than lumps of rock sticking out of the sea. Most references, however, agree that there are 700 significant islands and cays. As for the total number, some sources say there are 2,000, while other estimates are as high as 3,000. Such uncertainty may raise questions as to the total land area of the Bahamas, but officially it is 5,382 square miles (13,939 square km). The islands range in size from a tiny cay just a mile wide to Andros Island, the largest island in the Bahamas at 2,317 square miles (6,000 square km). The capital of the Bahamas, Nassau, is on the island of New Providence.

TOPOGRAPHY

The sea around the Bahamas is mostly shallow, although there are deep places such as the Tongue of the Ocean trench between Andros and the Exumas, which is more than a mile deep. The islands are quite low-lying, often no higher than 20 feet (6 m) and rarely exceeding 151 feet (46 m). The highest point, Mount Alvernia on Cat Island, is only 207 feet (63 m) high.

The majority of the Bahamian population live on fewer than 20 of the major islands. The most populated islands of the Bahamas, in order of population size, are New Providence, Grand Bahama, Eleuthera (including Harbour Island just offshore), the Abacos, Andros, the Exumas, Long Island, Cat Island, the Biminis, and the Inaguas.

Both Encyclopedia Britannica *and* The Random House Webster's College Dictionary *say the West Indies includes the Greater Antilles (Cuba, Dominican Republic, Haiti, Jamaica, and Puerto Rico), the Lesser Antilles, and the Bahamas. The dictionary defines the Caribbean as "the islands and countries of the Caribbean Sea," the sea being bound by Central America, the West Indies, and South America. By that definition, the Bahamas, as part of the West Indies, does not belong to the Caribbean.*

Politically, however, the Bahamas is included whenever the Caribbean as a collective entity is mentioned. For example, the Bahamas belongs to an intergovernmental organization called the Caribbean Development Bank, and it is a member of the Caribbean Community and Common Market (CARICOM for short). The Bahamas is also a beneficiary of the Caribbean Basin Initiative.

An underwater cave in the Bahamas.

THE BLUE HOLES The islands of the Bahamas sit on top of countless generations of sea fossils and disintegrated coral rising from the seabed. This sedimentary foundation, called oolitic limestone, is a soft rock that is easily eroded by mild acids such as rainwater. Over time, erosion has created sinkholes. Water-filled caves of the Bahamas are known as blue holes because of their colour.

Beneath the surface of some of the major islands is a subterranean world of caves filled with a combination of freshwater and seawater (seawater easily seeps through the limestone). These are the blue holes of the Bahamas. The blue holes have been explored extensively since the 1950s, when a Canadian, George Benjamin, began exploring the Andros caves. The famous underwater explorer Jacques Cousteau produced *The Jacques Cousteau Odyssey*, a television series with some episodes featuring the blue holes.

Explorations of the blue holes in the 1980s and 1990s revealed additional information. For example, in Grand Bahama, biologist Jill Yager discovered living species of a class of crustacean, remipedia, believed until then to have become extinct 150 million years ago. On Andros, skeletons and artifacts, including a Lucayan canoe believed to be

1,000 years old, were uncovered. (Lucayans were the natives who inhabited the Bahamas at the time of Christopher Columbus's landing.) In the process of exploration, more subterranean sites were discovered, including Zodiac Caverns on Grand Bahama Island and Stargate Blue Hole on South Andros, where Indian skulls were found during a National Geographic scuba-diving expedition in the early 1990s. Research is being conducted on how bacteria play a part in the formation of the caves. The blue holes were once sites for diving adventures, but now they have become frontiers of scientific study and research.

CLIMATE

The islands of the Bahamas lie in the path of the Gulf Stream, which helps maintain a uniform temperature year-round. A warm ocean current, the Gulf Stream flows northward from the Gulf of Mexico toward Newfoundland.

Dean's Blue Hole is the largest and deepest blue hole in the Bahamas.

Divers report a strange orange glow in the blue holes of the Bahamas. Scientists have explained that this is caused by the merging of freshwater and seawater. Seawater, being heavier, lies beneath freshwater. Where the two layers merge, a layer called halocline forms. Organic matter that sinks through freshwater settles in the halocline layer, where bacterial action causes it to break down. The halocline layer has a different chemical composition from the other two layers of water; it is more corrosive and typically orange.

Seats in the midst of the lush greens at the end of the casuarina grove on Little Whale Cay.

Winter lasts from mid-December to mid-April, with an average temperature of 67°F (19.5°C). Temperatures in summer (mid-April to mid-December) rarely exceed 81.5°F (27.5°C), since the trade winds blowing from the ocean keep the islands comparatively cool. There is little variation in the mean temperatures from north to south.

The average annual rainfall is 52 inches (132 cm), and relative humidity is 60-100 percent. The islands usually have only short tropical showers, but for six months, from June to November, Bahamians experience rainier weather; about 80 percent of the annual rainfall is in those months.

The Bahamas is just outside the Caribbean hurricane belt. In October 1996, Hurricane Lili battered resorts and devastated buildings and an airport tower. Hurricane Floyd hit the Bahamas on September 14, 1999, and Hurricane Michelle hit on November 4, 2001. Hurricane Noel came on October 28, 2007, and Tropical Storm Fay hit the Bahamas on August 15, 2008. With climate change and global warming, the intensity and frequency of hurricanes in the Bahamas is increasing.

FLORA

The Bahamas contains a significant amount of uncultivated land, due to extensive swamps. Centuries of decay of all kinds of vegetable matter on many of the islands have enriched the soil. As a result, although there is little lush vegetation, some of the islands, such as Andros and the Abacos, have forests of mahogany, ironwood, and pine. Lignum vitae, also called holywood, a hardwood with dark blue flowers, is the national tree. The original forests have been logged extensively to support boat-building and construction, as well as to clear land for plantations.

Bahamian plants include palms, ferns, bull vines, and some 30 to 40 wild orchid species. Mangrove plants, which can tolerate seawater, grow extensively in the swamps. Among plants introduced in the past century are Australian casuarinas; they were imported to prevent the erosion of sand dunes and are now part of the landscape. Fruit trees such as figs, tamarinds, and plums are also cultivated.

Watery clumps of green shrubs fill this mangrove forest in the Bahamas.

FAUNA

The Bahamas has two indigenous terrestrial mammals: the raccoon and the hutia, a species of guinea pig. Other animals were introduced over the years, and the wild horses, pigs, and donkeys living on some of the islands are descendants of domestic animals brought in by the early settlers. The Bahamian rock iguana, the Cat Island terrapin, the hawksbill turtle, and the green turtle are some of the reptiles and amphibians found in the Bahamas.

About 5 percent of the world's coral reefs are found in the Bahamas, enriching its variety of marine life. Marine biologists are attracted to the Bahamas because its seawater is especially clear, being devoid of the silt carried to the sea by rivers—there are no rivers in the Bahamas. Capitalizing on this and on the large numbers of dolphins found in the Bahamas and off the coast of Florida, the Wild Dolphin Project was founded by Dr. Denise Herzing in 1985 to study the behavior and social interactions of free-ranging Atlantic dolphins.

Caribbean sharks and other fishes in the Atlantic Ocean of the Bahamas.

A flock of flamingos stand on a beach along Great Inagua in the Bahamas. A diet of brine shrimp helps the flamingos maintain their brilliant pink color.

The Bahamas is a bird-watcher's paradise. The pink flamingo, the national bird, is found on all the islands, but Great Inagua has a flamingo rookery (a colony of birds) with more than 50,000 birds. Also quite common are roseate spoonbills, green parrots, hummingbirds, and herons. The Bahama parrot is a unique bird that nests in limestone cavities at ground level, making it vulnerable to predators such as wildcats that flourish in the Abaco forests. Abaco National Park is a protected nesting area and habitat for this endangered species.

Migratory birds include egrets, wild ducks, and wild geese. The islands are their winter home. Frigate birds, also called man-o'-war birds, frequent the Bahamas—airplane pilots have reported seeing these large seabirds flying as high as 8,005 feet (2,440 m)!

NEW PROVIDENCE

Although it is far from being the biggest island in the Bahamas, New Providence has the largest population, because the capital, Nassau, is located here. West of Nassau lies Cable Beach, one of the best-known coastal resorts in the Bahamas. The name commemorates the first telegraph cable, laid in 1892, linking Jupiter, Florida, to the Bahamas. The island has some of the country's major historical sites, but it is mainly the man-made attractions that draw

This panoramic view of Nassau shows the bridge linking New Providence and Paradise Island in the distance.

tourists and businesspeople. Nassau International Airport is located in the western half of New Providence.

Just 591 feet (180 m) across a small inlet from the city of Nassau lies the 692-acre (280-ha) Paradise Island, which originally went by the unromantic name of Hog Island. It was once privately owned; its first owner, William Sayle, bought it for $294. Paradise Island has been developed into a major resort complex, with many five-star hotels, casinos, and world-class golf courses. About 70 percent of all visitors to the Bahamas land first on either New Providence or Paradise Island.

NASSAU

Nassau, in northwestern New Providence, is the governmental, financial, and tourism center of the Bahamas. It has many architecturally interesting buildings, ranging from Victorian homes built by the British administrators of the islands to modern luxury apartments and resorts. It still retains a British flavor. The capital was founded in 1656 and named by its British rulers for King William III of England, one of whose titles was Prince of Nassau.

Among Nassau's numerous historical sites is the 18th-century Fort Charlotte, complete with a moat and dungeons. Another fort, Fort Fincastle, was designed to resemble a paddle-wheel steamer. The fort was converted into a lighthouse because of its location on the highest point of the island. Linking this fort to the Princess Margaret Hospital is the Queen's Staircase, a flight of 66 steps carved out of calcareous sandstone at the end of the 18th century. The Government House, the official residence of the British governor (today a ceremonial post), is an imposing pink-and-white building. The octagonal building that is the Nassau Public Library and Museum was once the city jail, and its small cells are now lined with bookshelves.

An aerial view of Nassau, with its numerous sea inlets and lush greens that make it one of the most popular spots in the Bahamas.

One of the oldest buildings in the city, the two-story Vendue House, was built in 1769 as a single-story slave market. It now houses the Pompey Museum, a cultural museum named to honor a slave who led several uprisings in the 1830s against his colonial masters on the island of Great Exuma. Also of historical significance is the Royal Victoria Gardens, the site of the Royal Victoria Hotel, which had been built in the 1860s in expectation of an influx of American tourists. The American Civil War dashed that hope, but it created another kind of boom for the hotel, attracting Confederate officers, Yankee spies, gunrunners, and reporters. The hotel closed in 1971, and shortly after that it burned down. Its ruins now make a vivid background for landscaped gardens.

The heart of the city is Rawson Square, which lies in the center of Bay Street. Close to the square is one of the largest straw markets in the world, where visitors can see all kinds of items woven from palmetto, a natural fiber obtained from young leafstalks of the cabbage palm tree. Popular palmetto products are baskets, rugs, and mats.

Bay Street, the city's main thoroughfare, contains shops that sell anything from duty-free Swiss watches to voodoo dolls to Chinese silk dresses. Bay Street is also the location of the biggest banks. The capital has become a significant offshore banking center in the Caribbean. Many of the world's major banks have outlets in Nassau that offer a wide variety of banking services to wealthy people drawn by the country's reputation as a tax-free haven.

Behind Bay Street is a wharf complex where cruise liners dock, bringing passengers from all over the world to experience Bahamian hospitality and buy souvenirs in the Bay Street shops. An interesting range of boats dock at the piers, from huge container ships to the small and often unique mail boats that are lifelines to outlying islands. Visitors can ride on mail boats to the nearby islands, so long as they don't need to stick to a strict schedule (a mail boat's schedule is quite flexible). Horse-drawn carriages known as surreys are a tourist attraction in Nassau. Their drivers—trained tour guides—take visitors around the major attractions of the city.

Vessels anchored at one of Nassau's many marinas.

GRAND BAHAMA

Grand Bahama in the north is the fourth-largest island in the Bahamian archipelago. The island is about 75 miles (120 km) long and 5 to 17 miles (8 to 27 km) wide. The northern shore is covered with mangrove swamps and wetlands; the southern shore is a long stretch of white beaches.

A scuba diver enjoys interacting with a dolphin in the waters surrounding Grand Bahama.

For many centuries Grand Bahama was visited, but never settled, by colorful characters ranging from Juan Ponce de León in 1513 (looking for the Fountain of Youth) to pirates in the 17th and 18th centuries. The first settlers came to Grand Bahama around 1841, but another century passed before anyone considered serious development there. West End is officially the capital of Grand Bahama, though Freeport is believed by many to be. West End is the oldest city and the westernmost settlement on the island. It first achieved notoriety as a rum-running port during Prohibition, the period from 1919 to 1933, during which the sale, manufacture, and transportation of alcohol for consumption was banned in the United States. Grand Bahama Island, being closest to the United States, was a convenient location for the rumrunners, who smuggled alcohol into the United States. The water surrounding Grand Bahama is incredibly clear, so the island has become a mecca for divers drawn by the fabulous variety of fish and some interesting shipwrecks. Several national parks are located here, including Lucayan National Park, which has a well-charted underwater cave system; Peterson Cay National Park; and the Rand Memorial Nature Center in the heart of Freeport, a bird-watcher's haven with a 1,969-foot (600-m) nature trail through a woods and a pine barrens. The curators lead educational bird-watching and wildflower tours every month. The Underwater Explorers Society (UNEXSO) offers "the Dolphin Experience" in Lucaya, where people interact with dolphins.

FREEPORT AND LUCAYA

Freeport is the second major city of the Bahamas, after Nassau. With its twin city, Lucaya, it was created by the rumrunners who made their homes and lucrative businesses there during Prohibition. As late as the 1950s, however, only about 4,000 people lived there.

In 1955, Wallace Groves, a Virginian financier with lumber interests on Grand Bahama, was granted 50,000 acres (20,230 ha) of pineyards with substantial areas of swamp and scrubland by the Bahamian government with a mandate to economically develop the area. A deepwater port was built to handle the growing lumber trade on the island, and the city of Freeport started to flourish. As of April 2007, premium waterfront lots could be brought for as little as 20 percent of the cost of their counterparts on the Florida coast. Construction in the Freeport area has picked up quickly as a result. An attractive feature of Freeport property is that it is covered by the Hawksbill Creek agreement. Under this agreement, personal real estate is tax-free until 2015.

Freeport has developed and grown tremendously since the 1950s. Together with Lucaya it has become the second-greatest tourist destination in the country, after Nassau. It offers major hotels, casinos, golf courses, and sport fishing. Freeport is planned on a grid with wide streets and widely separated buildings, giving people the impression that the city is less friendly, less "Bahamian" in character.

THE FAMILY ISLANDS

The Bahamas can be divided into three main regions: New Providence Island with the capital, Nassau; Grand Bahama; and the appropriately named Out Islands—all the other islands and cays. The government has renamed these the Family Islands, a name intended to give people a better perception of the islands, one that is inclusive and welcoming.

For centuries Family Islanders led a precarious existence through subsistence farming and fishing, their only link with the outside world the mail boat from Nassau. The Family Islands have their own schools and medical facilities, as well as local government. Many of them are developing their infrastructure to attract some of the lucrative tourist business currently

centered on New Providence and Grand Bahama. Most of them have access to the Internet, television, and radio. There are 19 Internet service providers in the Bahamas, a large number for a relatively small population.

THE ABACOS include Great Abaco, Little Abaco, and offshore cays with a 150-year-old reputation for boat-building. The first European settlers of the islands were American colonists fleeing the American Revolution. These original colonists made a modest living by salvaging wrecks, building small wooden boats, and basic farming. In Man-O-War Cay, boats are still handmade. There is an atmosphere of New England in the cays, particularly in New Plymouth and Hope Town, where a style of house called the saltbox is preserved. A saltbox house has just one story in the back and two stories in the front.

ACKLINS ISLAND AND CROOKED ISLAND, together with Long Cay, form an atoll enclosing a lagoon. This was once a favorite hideout of pirates, who ambushed ships passing through the Crooked Island Passage. The islands were settled by American Loyalists in the 18th century, but most of them left when their cotton plantations became uneconomical. Since 1999, Acklins and Crooked Island have been separate districts.

ANDROS, the largest island on the Bahamian archipelago, has some of the deepest blue holes. It is the least densely populated of all the major Bahamian islands, with a population of a little more than 6,000. Except

The Hope Town lighthouse and harbor of the Abacos, part of the Family Islands of the Bahamas.

An aerial view of Little Whale Cay, a private island within the Berry Islands in the Bahamas.

for the northeastern coast, where the bigger towns are located, the island is underdeveloped. The Atlantic Undersea Testing and Evaluation Center, a joint operation of the U.S. Navy and the Bahamian government, is located near Fresh Creek and is one of the busiest underwater testing facilities in the world.

BERRY ISLANDS is a group of 30 islands and nearly 100 cays. The islands attract mainly divers and beach lovers. Due to seasonal residents, the Berry Islands can boast of having more resident millionaires per unit area than any other place in the world.

THE BIMINIS consists of two islands: North Bimini is more populated, while South Bimini is the site of an airport. The legendary Fountain of Youth is supposed to be located near the airport.

CAT ISLAND is the only "highland" in the Bahamas, the country's highest point being Mount Alvernia. That is the site of a small monastery built by a Jesuit architect, Father Jerome.

ELEUTHERA was settled by English pilgrims in the 17th century. The main island is a destination for those interested in history and nature. Natural attractions include the Glass Window Bridge, the Hatchet Bay Caves, and Surfer's Beach in the north, and Ocean Hole and Lighthouse Beach at the south end.

THE EXUMAS are 365 cays stretched over 99 miles (160 km). The main islands are Great Exuma and Little Exuma, and the principal settlement is George Town. Exuma Cays Land and Sea Park is the world's first national park to lie partially submerged.

BEST BEACHES, GREAT DIVE SITES

The Bahamas has some of the most idyllic beaches in the world. The sand is fine and white and visible beneath shallow, crystal-clear water several yards out to sea. With more than 2,700 islands and cays, there are countless beaches to choose from. Among the most populated beaches are Old Fort Beach and Cable Beach on New Providence, Cabbage Beach on Paradise Island, Xanadu Beach on Grand Bahama, Tahiti Beach on the Abacos, Pink Sands Beach on Harbour Island, Ten Bay Beach on Eleuthera, and Saddle Cay on the Exumas. They are filled with opportunities for leisure sports and entertainment—water-skiing, windsurfing, snorkeling, beach bars, and restaurants. About 80 percent of Bahamian beaches are practically deserted, making them ideal for those who enjoy nature untouched by human activity and sounds.

The Bahamas is also a year-round diver's dream. There are dive sites for those who like exploring wrecks, but the main attraction is the marine life. Most of the islands are ringed with coral reefs—the reef off Andros is the third largest in the world. Dive sites have imaginative names: The Wall, Theo's Wreck, Spit City, Rose Garden, and Ben Blue Hole are some of them. Current Cut is an underwater gully that carries divers for a 10-minute ride on a swiftly flowing underwater current. Theo's Wreck dive site is named after the engineer, Theopolis Galanopoulos, who suggested scuttling the MS Logna in shallow waters as an attraction for scuba divers.

THE INAGUAS—two islands, Great Inagua and Little Inagua—have a harsh landscape, a hot climate, and little rainfall, all of which helps their major industry of salt production. Matthew Town, the capital, houses the Morton Salt Company's main facility, producing 1.1 million short tons (1 million metric tons) of sea salt a year—the second-largest solar saline operation in North America. Great Inagua is well known for its brilliant pink flamingos, which are protected in a vast reserve, Inagua National Park.

LONG ISLAND is aptly named, being 60 miles (97 km) long and only 4 miles (6 km) wide. Long Island is known as the most scenic island in the Bahamas. Cape Santa Maria Beach is listed among the most beautiful beaches in the world, and Dean's Blue Hole is the world's deepest blue hole, dropping to a depth of about 659 feet (201 m).

MAYAGUANA, the easternmost Bahamian island, is secluded. Most tourists who visit do so for the isolation, as well as for reef diving, bonefishing, snorkeling, and duck hunting. The eastern part of the island is popular with advanced off-trail bikers. Ecotourism is also a significant draw.

SAN SALVADOR was named by Christopher Columbus. The island remained off-limits to tourists until the late 1960s because of a secret military tracking station for nuclear missiles. When the U.S. military, no longer seeing a need for the station, left the island in the late 1960s, it left an infrastructure of well-constructed buildings, an electrical power station, and a paved air strip, which are now used by the Bahamas government.

One of the last kerosene lighthouses in the world can be found on the island of San Salvador in the Bahamas.

Inagua is an anagram for *iguana,* the herbivorous lizard found on Bahamian beaches. However, *inagua* is believed to be derived from the Spanish *lleno* ("full") and *agua* ("water").

NATIONAL PARKS—A NATIONAL TRUST

In 1959, to save the West Indian flamingo from extinction, the Bahamas National Trust was created by an act of parliament. As a result, Exuma Cays Land and Sea Park was established—a 176-square-mile (456-square-km) marine reserve for tropical birds and the Bahamian iguana. By the end of the millennium, the trust had created 11 more national parks, covering hundreds of thousands of acres of wetlands and forests, to protect the country's biodiversity and natural resources. As part of its conservation responsibilities, the trust formulates the national strategy for environment and development, makes recommendations for ecotourism, conducts independent studies of projects such as resort developments that impact on the environment, contributes the environmental component to the national education curriculum, and participates in numerous international conferences on environmental issues.

PROTECTING WILDLIFE

The Bahamas is a member of the Convention on International Trade in Endangered Species of Wild Flora and Fauna (CITES), which was created in 1973 to protect wildlife against exploitation of species on a scale that threatens its existence. In accordance with CITES rules, the Bahamas has divided its endangered species into two groups: those near extinction and those likely to become endangered. No trade is allowed in the first category, while limited trade is permitted for the second.

Among the species nearing extinction are peregrine falcons, Bahama parrots, four species of turtles (loggerhead, hawksbill, green, and leatherback turtles), Bahamian rock iguanas, American crocodiles, whales, dolphins, and West Indian manatees.

The Ministry of Agriculture is the CITES managing authority in the Bahamas, while the Bahamas National Trust acts as the scientific authority. Together these organizations grant permits for trade in endangered species and educate people on the need to preserve wildlife, particularly endangered species.

The national parks run by the trust protect diverse species and at the same time offer eco-related activities such as bird-watching and nature walks. In the Abacos, a parrot haven was created in Abaco National Park, while Black Sound Cay National Reserve is a waterfowl habitat. Conception Island National Park is a sanctuary for migratory birds, a rookery for seabirds, and an egg-laying site for the green turtle. Green turtles also visit the Union Creek Reserve on Great Inagua, a 7-square-mile (18-square-km) enclosed tidal creek that is a breeding research site for giant sea turtles. This reserve is known worldwide as the nesting ground for the largest colony of wild West Indian flamingos—about 60,000 of them. Plants are not forgotten. In the middle of Nassau's residential area, the headquarters of the trust is set amid 11 acres (4.5 ha) of botanical gardens and 200 species of palm trees, the largest private collection in the West Indies.

Among the parks, Lucayan National Park in Grand Bahama is special: It has the longest—6 miles (10 km)—charted underwater cave system in the world. Ongoing scientific studies here have contributed to a greater understanding of the chemistry of similar limestone caves. Pelican Cays Land and Sea Park in the Abacos is another site known for undersea caves.

HISTORY

Amid the lush green Versailles Gardens on Paradise Island stands The Cloisters, a 14th-century French monastery imported stone by stone from Europe and transplanted atop a hill in the 1960s.

MANY SPECIFIC EVENTS in history contribute to our understanding of any country. For the Bahamas, some of these events began elsewhere, before many of the islands were populated.

THE LUCAYANS

At least 500 years before the Europeans arrived in the New World, the Bahamas was inhabited by a gentle race of people called the Lucayans. They were descendants of the Arawak Indians, who originally lived in northern South America, throughout the islands of the Caribbean, and

as far north as present-day Florida. The Lucayans had gradually been driven northward by the Carib tribe, a warlike people, whose practice of cannibalism made them very much feared by the peaceable Lucayans. The highly developed Lucayan culture boasted its own language, government, religion, craft traditions, and extensive trade routes. Although the Lucayans had weapons, such as bows and poison-tipped arrows, they had not developed armor to protect themselves.

"Lucayans" was Columbus's name for the native Arawaks who lived on the island where he first touched land in the New World.

For centuries the Lucayans lived a simple life in villages throughout the Bahamas, subsisting mainly on fish caught with bone fishhooks and growing corn and cassava root for food. They also grew cotton, which they spun and wove into hammocks. These attracted the attention of the first Europeans to visit the Bahamas, as hammocks provided a comfortable alternative to the hard decks of their ships.

The Lucayans traveled in big canoes carved out of mahogany logs. In 1996 mapmaker Bob Gascoine was working in a mangrove swamp at North Creek on Grand Turk Island. Suddenly the propeller of his boat struck a submerged object. Curious, Gascoine investigated the sound and found he had run over what looked like an odd reddish stick poking out the mud. An amateur archaeologist, Gascoine recognized that this was not a stick but a Lucayan canoe paddle. He hastily summoned the museum, and the paddle was removed to a stable environment.

The Guanahani Landfall Park is a replica of a Lucayan village at the time of Colombus's arrival in 1492.

CHRISTOPHER COLUMBUS

On October 12, 1492, Christopher Columbus stepped ashore on a little island that the Lucayans called Guana-hani. He immediately renamed it San Salvador and claimed it for Spain. The Lucayans welcomed Columbus and his men, from whom they saw no threat. In fact, initially there was no threat, because the coral islands had no economic value. Columbus was looking for gold and a passage to China.

When Columbus arrived with his crew, the Lucayans welcomed them with food.

After some time on the islands, which he later described as being among the most beautiful he had ever seen, Columbus sailed south toward Cuba. At the time of Columbus's arrival in 1492, there were five Taíno kingdoms and territories on Hispaniola (the island that is home to Haiti and Dominican Republic). It is believed that the seafaring Taínos were relatives of the South American Arawaks. Their language belonged to the Maipurean linguistic family, which ranges from South America across the Caribbean. Taíno religion centered on the worship of cemís. Cemís are gods, spirits, or ancestors.

Columbus's expedition discovered gold on Hispaniola. Before the gold was exhausted, however, the Taíno natives died from overwork at the hands of the Spanish or foreign diseases against which they had little immunity. Remembering the Lucayans, the Spanish sent an expedition to San Salvador to round them up and bring them to Hispaniola. About 20,000 Lucayans were killed for resisting or subdued and shipped to Hispaniola to work. Approximately 25 years after Christopher Columbus discovered San Salvador, the Lucayan society in the Bahamas no longer existed.

SLEEPING ISLANDS

The Bahamian islands attracted fortune seekers such as Ponce de León (c. 1460-1521).

The Bahamian islands came under the nominal control of Spain after Columbus's visit, an arrangement formalized under the Treaty of Tordesillas between Spain and Portugal in 1494. The Treaty of Tordesillas divided the "newly discovered" lands outside Europe between the two countries along a meridian about halfway between the Cape Verde Islands (already Portuguese), off the west coast of Africa, and the islands "discovered" by Columbus on his first voyage. These islands were named in the treaty as Cipangu and Antilia (Cuba and Hispaniola) and claimed by Spain. The lands to the east would belong to Portugal and the lands to the west to Spain.

For more than a century, however, the Bahamian islands were seldom visited, much less settled. From time to time explorers would wander into the shallow seas, then move on. One such visitor was Juan Ponce de León, a Spanish conqueror looking for the fabled Fountain of Youth. Other Europeans passed through, including the Dutch and the French. British explorers such as John Cabot and John Hawkins also visited the Bahamas during the 1500s, but they too did not stay. All these explorers were very likely discouraged by the treacherous reefs surrounding many of the islands.

It was not until 1629 that anyone thought seriously about settling the Bahamas. In that year, ignoring the Spanish claim, King Charles I of England granted to his attorney general, Sir Robert Heath, the right to establish settlements in territories in America including "Bahama" and all the islands lying south or near the continent. This right was never exercised; the islands were too far away, and besides, Charles I had major problems in England, which ended with his execution in 1649. (Robert Heath fled to France.)

Meanwhile, conflict between the Puritans and the Anglican Church in England caused the Puritans to leave for North America and other territories, among them the Bermuda islands, which England had colonized in 1612.

THE ELEUTHERIAN ADVENTURERS

Old World religious influence soon reached the New World, and in the Bermudas some oppressed Puritans decided it was time to move on. In 1647 William Sayle formed the Company of Eleutherian Adventurers, whose goal was to look for an island where they would be free to establish plantations and worship as they wished. In the summer of 1648, Sayle and 70 other Puritans arrived at what is now Governor's Harbour on the island of Cigatoo, now known as Eleuthera, and became the first group of Europeans to take up residence in the Bahamas.

The newcomers had a rocky start. Even before they arrived, one of their two ships was wrecked. They sent the other ship out for provisions. To survive in the long term, however, they needed more than provisions. Rich soil was necessary for farming, but the island's coralline base was covered by only a thin layer of poor soil. Consequently many of their farming projects failed. For a few years Sayle traveled in search of funds. Fellow Puritans who had settled in the new colony of Massachusetts on the American mainland collected funds in exchange for amber and timber. The Eleutherian Adventurers also survived by scavenging from the numerous vessels wrecked on the coral reefs surrounding the island. Despite their efforts, the settlement could not survive. About 10 years after they first landed,most of the Eleutherian Adventurers had returned to Bermuda, among them William Sayle.

An engraving by King Charles I allowing Robert Heath the right to establish settlements along the Caribbean.

The chief settlement on New Providence was called Charles Town in 1660, in honor of King Charles II. When William of Nassau, better known as King William III of England, ascended the throne, the settlers renamed this settlement Nassau to honor him.

Meanwhile, another group of Bermudans arrived on New Providence, west of Eleuthera, in 1656. The soil there was a little better. Quite independent of this, Sayle had also been interested in New Providence, having sheltered there during one of his northward journeys. In 1663, when he was appointed governor of South Carolina, he took every opportunity to speak glowingly to the British about the Bahamas. As a result, in 1670 the Duke of Albemarle and five other Englishmen were granted proprietorship of the islands by King Charles II. They appointed a governor in 1671, then left the islands to their fate, contributing nothing to development beyond a succession of governors who were lazy and corrupt.

The year 1671 was also the first time a census was ever taken in the Bahamas. There were 1,097 residents, 443 of whom were originally slaves brought in from Africa to work on the British cotton, tobacco, sugarcane, and sisal plantations.

The neglect of the British proprietors left the islands open to attack by pirates. Given little protection, many of the settlers fled, leaving the Bahamian islands wide open once again to anyone who wanted to live there. Many pirates actually settled on the islands.

The early travelers faced many dangers in the Bahamas; shipwrecks were a common occurrence.

PIRACY

The protected bays throughout the Bahamian islands were ideal places to conceal pirate ships and intercept passing vessels. The British governors who were supposed to be enforcing the law were often in league with the pirates, including such notorious characters as Edward Teach (Blackbeard), Mary Read, and Anne Bonny. There was no significant change for the next 30 years. If anything, the situation worsened, as Nassau was attacked a few times by the Spanish in retaliation for the loss of ships to pirates.

A CROWN COLONY

The settlers from Britain made a case for Crown control, and they succeeded in 1717 when the proprietors surrendered their rights to King George I of Britain. In 1718 Captain Woodes Rogers was appointed the first royal governor of the Bahamas. By this time more than 1,000 pirates were living on New Providence alone. Rogers began the long and difficult task of getting rid of

Anne Bonny and Mary Read dressed like men and were as vicious as their male pirate mates.

WOODES ROGERS, an Englishman who went to sea to be a sailor, became a pirate buster when he assumed command of an expedition sponsored by merchants of Bristol, England, to eliminate piracy and make the shipping routes safe for their trading vessels. In 1709 his ship rescued a man called Alexander Selkirk from the Pacific island on which he was marooned; this adventure inspired Daniel Defoe to write Robinson Crusoe. In 1718 the king of England appointed Rogers governor of the Bahamas with a specific command: to rid the islands of nearly 2,000 pirates who lived there. Rogers succeeded in this difficult task. In 1729 he called the first meeting of the House of Assembly, which passed 12 acts of parliament designed to bring law and order to the islands of the Bahamas. By the time he died in the Bahamas in 1732, the days of pirate control of the islands were over.

ANNE BONNY was born in County Cork, Ireland. She came to North America when her father, a lawyer, moved his family to the Carolinas to start a plantation. At a quite young age she married a sailor, James Bonny, who took her to the Bahamas where he worked for Governor Woodes Rogers in the fight against piracy. Anne fell in love with one of the enemy, Calico Jack. Late one night Calico Jack and Anne Bonny stole a ship moored in the Nassau harbor and sailed away to begin a life of piracy together. She dressed like a man, became an expert with the pistol and the cutlass, and came to be considered as dangerous as any male pirate. In 1720 Calico Jack's ship, the Revenge, was attacked by a British vessel, and all its crew, including Anne Bonny and fellow pirate Mary Read, were captured. Bonny and Read were sentenced to death, but both confessed to their gender and were spared an immediate hanging due to the fact that they were pregnant. Mary Read died in jail, but Anne Bonny, after several postponements of her execution, simply disappeared. What happened to her remains unknown, but most people think her father managed to arrange her escape and that she returned to the Carolinas to live out the rest of her life under an assumed name.

them. His method was ingenious: He pardoned some of them to get their cooperation so that he could capture others. Some pirates were sent to England for trial, and some were executed in the Bahamas, but by 1732, when Rogers died in Nassau, the situation was finally under control, and the settlers could begin to live and work without the constant fear of attack from either the Spanish or the pirates. In 1741 there were more than 2,000 settlers in the Bahamas.

Rogers also ordered strong forts to be built to repel attacks from ships. He used these effectively against the Spanish in 1720. In 1729 Rogers organized an assembly of representatives to govern the islands. Thus began more orderly government and the beginning of commerce.

THE LOYALISTS ARRIVE

The American Revolution brought significant changes to the peaceful Bahamian islands. When the war ended with the British defeat, many of the settlers in the former British colonies of North America immigrated to neighboring areas still controlled by the British. They were known as Loyalists because they had supported the English king. After Canada, the Bahamas was the most popular destination because of its warm climate and its proximity to the United States. As a result, the population of the islands tripled during the 1780s with the arrival of more than 8,000 Loyalists and their slaves.

The Loyalist settlers were mostly farming people from the southern United States. With their arrival, new cotton plantations began to spring up in the Bahamas, worked by the slaves they brought with them. Unfortunately the plantations did not prosper, mainly due to the chenille bug and soil exhaustion. Many settlers eventually emigrated, some to resettle on more-fertile British Caribbean islands such as Barbados, others to return to the United States. Those who stayed eventually did quite well for themselves by branching into other occupations, including fishery and boatbuilding. Remnants of Loyalist communities are still found on the islands, their homes

This monument in the Sculpture Garden on Green Turtle Cay in New Plymouth honors Loyalist pioneers and their descendants.

THE AMERICAN REVOLUTION AND THE BAHAMAS

The Bahamas has a strategic location between North and South America. On at least three occasions in the 18th century, during the war between Britain and the American colonies, the Bahamas was invaded by foreign troops: twice by Americans and once by the Spanish. All three invasions ended after a temporary occupation by foreign forces.

__1776 AND 1778:__ The American Revolution closely affected the Bahamas because there were family ties with the residents of the British colonies and consequently some sympathy for the cause of American independence. When the American navy attacked the Bahamas in 1776, however, it was not at the urging of sympathizers but because Fort Nassau had a cache of gunpowder that the Americans badly needed. (Britain had imposed a blockade of the northern colonies, preventing the entry of arms and ammunition.) Unfortunately for the Americans, the gunpowder had been spirited away before they arrived. The rebels had a very good time in the islands despite not finding any gunpowder and parted company with the Bahamians on excellent terms two weeks later.

__1782:__ Taking advantage of the fact that the British forces were busy fighting a war in the north, the Spanish attacked and occupied Nassau in 1782. A Loyalist colonel, Andrew Deveaux, tricked the Spanish into surrender in a particularly hilarious way: He used a boat and one band of 200 mercenaries and sailed them into the harbor (and then out) over and over again so that the Spanish were fooled into believing themselves outnumbered. Ironically this strategy was unnecessary, since the Spanish ceded the Bahamas to England in the Peace of Versailles in January 1783.

in the architectural styles they brought with them. Several Bahamian family names can be traced to the Loyalist settlers. In the Exumas, for example, many residents are called Rolle after their slave ancestors who adopted the name of their master, Denys Rolle.

The slave population increased to more than 12,000 by the start of the 1800s. The social system in the Bahamas began to change in this period, beginning with the abolition of the slave trade throughout the British Empire in 1807 and the total emancipation of slaves in 1834. Indentured labor and universal education were introduced.

BLOCKADE RUNNING

For most of the 19th century the Bahamian islands were tranquil, although not very prosperous owing to few trading opportunities. Most families lived on subsistence farming. The outbreak of the American Civil War in 1861 brought a new activity: blockade running, which became a very profitable business.

Early in the Civil War, President Abraham Lincoln imposed a blockade on the American South to starve it into submission. The Bahamians supplied the Southern states with the manufactured goods they needed but could no longer obtain through the Northern ports of the United States. At the same time Bahamians marketed the cotton exports of these states in Nassau. Many Bahamians had special fast ships built to make their fortunes evading the gunships of the Yankee army enforcing the blockade. The Royal Victoria Hotel, which had just been built to house an expected influx of American tourists to Nassau, instead became a center for the blockade runners and quickly earned a reputation as the place to party every night.

The excitement and prosperity of the Civil War years ended with the surrender of the Confederacy in 1865, and the Bahamas returned to its tranquil, peaceful existence. New opportunities emerged only to fail. For example, conch shells became a good trade item for a while until the fashion for them died. Early civilizations in the pre-Columbian period used the shell as a horn for religious ceremonies, for trade and ornamentation, and for bracelets, hairpins, and necklaces. The trade in sponges prospered until they were all killed by a fungus. Although marine sponges have been sought after since ancient times, industrialisation created a growing demand for them in the cleaning, ceramics, shoe-finishing, and printing industries in addition to household, bathing, and medical uses. The invention of synthetic substitutes after the war sharply reduced demand for natural sponges. The pineapple-canning factories, which had been established in the Bahamas with

Seated on a heap of sponges, a Bahamian prepares a consignment for export as the sponge trade nears its end in the early 20th century.

World War I badly damaged the economy of the islands, which was still strongly linked to that of Britain. The Bahamas had little real contact with the war, but the people proved themselves to be British patriots by contributing lives and funds to the war effort.

high expectations, began to fail after the American government put a punitive import tax on pineapples entering the United States. The citrus fruit crops met the same fate.

PROHIBITION BOOM

As Florida began to develop, many Bahamians left to settle there, with mixed results for the Bahamas. On the positive side, new communication links were established with the booming city of Miami—first a regular steamship service, then a telegraph connection, and after 1931, radio links. One negative result was the depletion of the population in the Bahamas.

The Duke and Duchess of Windsor were popular with the people of the Bahamas.

Salvation came with the advent of Prohibition in 1919. For the next 14 years the Bahamas supplied illegal alcohol to speakeasies (places selling drinks illegally) all over the United States. The good old days of blockade running began again, and many Bahamians made fortunes operating small, fast boats that outran the U.S. Coast Guard and delivered whisky, gin, rum, and beer to the many inlets dotting the eastern Florida coast. When Prohibition ended in 1933, the Bahamas succumbed to the Depression, which had already affected people elsewhere.

A TAX REFUGE

It was a millionaire this time who saved the Bahamas. In 1934, Sir Harry Oakes, who had made his fortune in Canadian gold mines, found the Bahamas a good place to live, both for its climate and for its hands-off attitude toward the taxes he should be paying on his fortune. He told his friends about this attractive tax haven, and the Bahamas began to gain popularity among the wealthy for permanent residence. Among those who could not afford to live there it became known as a beautiful place to visit.

The appointment of the Duke of Windsor, the former king of England who had abdicated to marry a divorcée, as the governor of the Bahamas in 1940 added to the attraction of the Bahamas during World War II, for the duke was a popular man. He instituted economic reforms and was instrumental in the building of an air base on New Providence to train pilots during the war. The Bahamas also became important as a strategic base for antisubmarine warfare against the Germans. Two airports built during the war to support the Allied forces based there later provided the infrastructure for the postwar tourism boom.

After the war ended the Bahamians took advantage of the facilities left behind by the British to develop the tourist industry in a big way. This was timely, for by then the attitude of the middle classes to leisure had changed, and more people who were not rich were traveling for pleasure. Then, in the early 1960s, after Cuba became communist and the United States imposed an embargo on that country, tourists looking for a new destination discovered the perfect alternative in the Bahamas.

INDEPENDENCE

The Bahamians had been in control of their internal government since Woodes Rogers established an assembly of representatives in 1729, but sovereignty was still held by the British Crown. This meant that the Bahamas was a colony of the British Empire, but its own politicians were able to make most decisions with regards to the running of the Bahamas without reference to the British Crown. In 1963, during a conference in London, it was agreed that the Bahamas should be given self-government. The process began with a new constitution in 1964 and the first general election to choose a prime minister and a cabinet.

In 1967, after the second election, in which the first black prime minister was elected, the Bahamas achieved full self-government. This meant that it administered it own internal affairs but was not fully sovereign or independent yet. The United Kingdom still retained control of foreign affairs, defense, and internal security. The Bahamas became fully independent on July 10, 1973, when its nominally adopted name of Commonwealth of the Bahama Islands was changed to Commonwealth of the Bahamas.

The emancipation of slaves in the Bahamas was painless compared with the situation in the American South. This is possibly because the Bahamian plantations had failed, and slaves were no longer essential; instead, their welfare was a financial burden. By the time of the American Civil War, the population of the Bahamas was mostly black.

GOVERNMENT

The stately Parliament Building in Nassau, where government meetings take place.

CHAPTER 3

FOR 250 YEARS, from 1723 to 1973, the Bahamas was a colony of the United Kingdom, and all the important decisions affecting the growth of the country and the welfare and taxation of the Bahamian people were made on the other side of the Atlantic Ocean, in London.

There was a brief period during the American Revolutionary War when the Bahamas fell to Spanish forces under General Bernardo de Gálvez in 1782. A British-American Loyalist expedition later recaptured the islands. The governors of the Bahamas enjoyed local authority after 1729, but until recently they were required to refer any major decisions to the British Colonial Office, and through that to the British Parliament.

As recently as the early 1950s, there were no political parties in the Bahamas, and Bahamians had no official body to express their concerns and wishes about the way the islands were governed. Twenty years later, however, the Bahamas had become a fully independent, sovereign country, with a government authorized by the electorate to decide on every aspect of government, including foreign relations and defense.

Today the Bahamas is a parliamentary democracy and a member of the Commonwealth of Nations, a group of countries once governed by the United Kingdom. However, the Bahamas has retained the British monarch, Queen Elizabeth II, as its head

Queen Elizabeth II presides over the State Opening of Parliament during her visit to the Bahamas in 1977.

of state. She is represented by a Bahamian-born governor-general whom she appoints on the advice of the prime minister of the Bahamas.

This chapter examines significant events after World War II and popular attitudes that shaped modern politics in the Bahamas. It also describes the political parties, the current structure of government, the important features of the Bahamian constitution, and other organizations that support the functions of the government.

POSTWAR POLITICAL CHANGES

The changing-of-the-guard ceremony at Government House is performed with pomp and pageantry every other Saturday morning in Nassau.

Long before World War II, the political assembly had been in the hands of the white merchants and lawyers known as the Bay Street Boys. The term was derogatory, for this group was blamed for practically everything that went wrong in the Bahamian economy. The Bay Street Boys dismissed the blacks as a political force. But during the war, thousands of them lost their lives, a point that some blacks drove home to their compatriots. This was the beginning of a shift in the political power base.

In 1953 a group led by Lynden O. Pindling founded the Progressive Liberal Party (PLP), with a political platform of improving the social, economic, and political situation in the Bahamas. The Bay Street Boys reacted by forming the United Bahamian Party (UBP) in 1958. Britain sent the secretary of state for the colonies to the Bahamas to determine the grassroots political sentiment, and as a result of his recommendations, the 1960s was a time of great political change in the Bahamas.

In 1964 a new Bahamian constitution was adopted, the first-ever specifically for the Bahamas itself. It replaced the colonial government structure with a two-chamber parliament elected by Bahamians and headed by a prime minister and a cabinet whose members were drawn from the political party with the most votes. The British Parliament continued to appoint a governor to look after British interests in the Bahamas, but now he acted only in consultation with the prime minister.

The UBP, led by Roland Symonette, won the first election by a narrow majority. The opposition in parliament, led by Lynden Pindling, adopted a political strategy of disobedience that climaxed in its boycott of parliament in 1967. This forced another election, and Pindling became the first black prime minister of the Bahamas.

He began the process of leading the country toward total independence from the United Kingdom. In 1969 changes to the constitution gave the Bahamas self-government, and only defense, foreign relations, and internal security remained with the British government.

Not all Bahamians wanted independence. Many felt there was no need to hurry the process, among them the Free National Movement (FNM), a 1971 coalition of the UBP and dissident members of the PLP. By majority vote, however, the electorate decided the issue when they elected Pindling for a second term in 1972.

A constitutional conference was called in London to discuss the proposal for complete independence. As a result of the London talks a new constitution for the Bahamas was drawn up. At midnight on July 9, 1973, the birth of the independent nation of the Bahamas was symbolically recognized by the lowering of the Union Jack (the British flag) and the raising of the new Bahamian flag in Nassau.

The Commonwealth secretary, George Thomson, addresses the Bahamas Constitutional Conference in London, while Lynden Pindling, then prime minister of the Bahamas, seated opposite, listens attentively.

THE CONSTITUTION

The 1973 constitution of the Commonwealth of the Bahamas proclaims the country to be a sovereign democratic state. It also establishes the executive, legislative, and judicial branches of government and creates the Public Service Commission, the Judicial and Legal Commission, and the Police

The Supreme Courts in Nassau (*above*) and Freeport are presided over by the chief justice or one of seven other justices appointed by the governor-general.

The motto of the Royal Bahamas Police Force is "Courage Integrity Loyalty."

Service Commission. The constitution also guarantees fundamental rights and freedoms and the protection of these rights under the law without discrimination based on race, national origin, political opinion, color, creed, or gender. The constitution may be amended only by an act of parliament in combination with a popular referendum.

GOVERNMENT STRUCTURE

The governor-general appointed by the British monarch plays a ceremonial role. The actual business of governing is conducted by the Bahamian parliament. This body has two chambers: the Senate and the House of Assembly. The Senate has 16 members appointed by the governor-general: nine on the advice of the prime minister, four on the advice of the leader of the opposition, and three on the advice of the prime minister after consultation with the leader of the opposition. The House of Assembly is composed of at least 38 members elected by the citizenry (the legal voting age is 18) at least every five years. The number of Assembly members may be increased by the Constituencies Commission, which reviews electoral boundaries every five years. The most recent election, on May 2, 2007, increased the number of members to 41. The executive branch of government is the cabinet, which has at least nine ministers, including the prime minister and the attorney general. The prime minister appoints the other cabinet members.

The constitution requires laws to be enacted by parliament in a certain manner: A bill is introduced in the House of Assembly, read three times, and debated. If it is passed, it becomes an act. The act is read three times in the Senate and then sent to the governor-general. When he has signed the act, it is published in the official journal of the government and becomes a law.

THE JUSTICE SYSTEM

The justice system is modeled on the British common-law system but includes Bahamian statute law. Many members of the legal profession in the Bahamas have trained in and are eligible to practice in Britain. The judiciary is independent of government control.

The hierarchy of courts ranges from local magistrate's courts in New Providence and Grand Bahama to the Supreme Courts (one each in Nassau and Freeport) and the Court of Appeal. There is also the right of appeal to Her Majesty's Privy Council in England.

Appeals move upward; for example, an appeal from a decision of a Family Island commissioner is heard in a magistrate's court, while an appeal from a decision in a magistrate's court is heard in the Supreme Court. The attorney general and the Bahamas Bar Association constantly review the Bahamian justice system.

DEFENSE AND POLICE FORCES

The Bahamas has no army or navy. Its Royal Bahamas Defense Force performs mainly the duties of a coast guard service, which include the extremely difficult task of intercepting smugglers who operate in the waters surrounding the islands. The Royal Bahamas Police Force is responsible for the maintenance of law and order everywhere in the Bahamas.

The police are the main enforcers of the law in Bahamas.

LYNDEN O. PINDLING *(1930—2000) from Nassau was the prime minister of the Bahamas from 1967 to 1992. He made history in 1967 by becoming the first black Bahamian prime minister, leading the Progressive Liberal Party to victory against the United Bahamian Party. Pindling led the country to full independence and instituted reforms that transformed banking and investment management into major industries. In 1983 he was knighted by Queen Elizabeth II. From the 1980s, however, his government was the target of allegations of corruption, particularly of accepting bribes from drug syndicates and improper loans from businesspeople. These charges, added to the country's high inflation and unemployment, led to the defeat of his party in the 1992 election. In 1997, after the landslide victory of the Free National Movement party, Pindling resigned as leader of the PLP.*

HUBERT ALEXANDER INGRAHAM *(1947—) grew up in Coopers Town on Great Abaco. He qualified as a lawyer in 1972. In 1975 he entered politics as a member of the ruling Progressive Liberal Party and was elected to the House of Assembly in 1977. After his reelection in 1982 he became the minister of Housing, National Insurance, and Social Services. Two years later he was dismissed from the cabinet when he protested against government corruption, and in 1986 he was expelled from the PLP altogether. In the 1987 general election Ingraham ran as an independent candidate and was elected to the House of Assembly. He joined the official opposition to the PLP in April 1990 and was appointed leader of the Free National Movement in May. Ingraham revitalized the FNM and in 1992 led his party to an overwhelming victory over the PLP, ending its 25-year control of the Bahamian government. He was reelected in 2007 with a 2.84 percent margin and a five-seat majority for his party in the House of Assembly. In addition to being the prime minister, Ingraham is responsible for trade and industry. He has pledged to stamp out all corruption in the Bahamas and to conduct government affairs "in the sunshine."*

LEADERSHIP CHANGES

Lynden Pindling was prime minister from 1967 until 1992, leading the Progressive Liberal Party. Toward the end of his last term in office, Bahamians were growing increasingly unhappy with his government's corrupt practices. Not surprisingly, the Free National Movement was voted into power in 1992, led by Hubert Alexander Ingraham. The FNM majority in 1992 was a slender 56 percent. The 1997 election saw a significant increase to 85 percent, for by then it was clear that the FNM's policies were helping the country recover after 25 years of mismanagement. Ingraham lost to a resurgent PLP, under the leadership of his former law partner Perry Christie, in 2002. Ingraham turned leadership of the FNM over to Orville "Tommy" Turnquest in 2002, but in 2007 he returned to lead the FNM to victory again by a five-seat margin, and he is the prime minister once again.

To reduce the $1.1 billion national debt it inherited in the early 1990s, the FNM offered an attractive incentive package to foreign investors and homeowners. The National Investment Policy encouraged the privatization of government-run businesses to reduce the government's financial burden. With prudent policies, the debt was reduced to $358 million by 1996, inflation was brought down from 3 percent in 1985 to 0.5 percent in 1997, and unemployment was reduced from 17 to 22 percent in the mid-1980s to around 10 percent by 1997. Debt was reduced even further, to $342.6 million by 2004, inflation was about 2.4 percent in 2007, and unemployment was 7.6 percent in 2006.

The Bahamas's Prime Minister Hubert Ingraham.

ECONOMY

The Bahamas Financial Centre in Nassau.

A S A HIGH-INCOME COUNTRY, the Bahamas has been disqualified from receiving World Bank loans since 1988. The average annual income per Bahamian was $28,600 in 2008. Over the years, many products and services have earned income for the Bahamas, but the country has always been a much larger importer than exporter.

The Bahamian economy is almost entirely dependent on tourism and financial services to generate foreign exchange earnings. Tourism alone

Christopher Columbus said of the Bahamas that "the beauty of these islands surpasses that of any other and as much as the day surpasses the night in splendor." Not surprisingly, the Bahamas is a favorite tourist destination for Americans and Europeans.

The colorful Carnival Crystal Palace resort in Nassau, along with the many other resorts found in the Bahamas, draws many tourists and boosts the local economy.

provides an estimated 60 percent of the country's gross domestic product (GDP) and employs about half of the Bahamian workforce. Privatization of formerly government-run companies is part of the government's economic strategy. This has encouraged home ownership by foreigners, creating a construction boom, and even the sale of islands. Despite its interest in foreign investment to diversify the economy, however, the Bahamian government responds to local concerns about foreign competition and tends to protect local business and labor interests. At the same time, domestic resistance to foreign investment and high labor costs can cause growth to stagnate in sectors that the government wishes to diversify.

TOURISM

"It's better in the Bahamas" is a slogan of the Ministry of Tourism. Tourism dominates the Bahamian economy. In 1999, 3.65 million people visited the islands, with 2.2 million of them arriving by cruise ship. Revenue from tourism made up 60 percent of the nation's GDP. The average tourist spent

An aerial view of the pools in the Atlantis resort.

$958 while vacationing in the Bahamas, and tourist spending overall amounted to $1.5 billion in 2008. In 2000, about 81,700 Bahamians were employed in the tourist industry. Most visitors are from the United States (83 percent in 1999). The country's tourism ministry, one of the most effective in the world, has offices in the United States, Canada, and Europe to market the Bahamas as a tourist destination. All major cruise lines operate services to the Bahamas. To extend the stay of passengers, the government has enacted legislation that allows ships to open their casinos and stores only if they remain in port for more than 18 hours.

Tourism has been a major thrust for the government since the Royal Victoria Hotel was built in Nassau to attract American tourists in the mid-19th century. It was only after World War II ended, though, that government efforts to promote tourism increased significantly. New Providence is the main tourist destination and has seen many hotel and casino developments, particularly in the past decade. The largest resort on the island is the 2,340-room Atlantis, which is owned by Sun International. It employs 5,500 people and is the second-largest employer in the nation, after the government. Other major resorts on the island include Club Med (popular with the French), Sandals (attracting the British), and Holiday Inn. The Grand Bahama Development Company plans to spend $50 million upgrading airport and cruise ship facilities to accommodate an additional 555,000 visitors a year.

Similar but smaller-scale tourism developments are taking place on some of the other Bahamian islands in an effort to attract more foreign tourists, especially during the winter months. The town of Freeport on Grand Bahama is being developed into a major tourism and business center. As of April 2007, premium waterfront lots could be brought for as little as 20 percent of the cost of their counterparts on the Florida coast. Construction in the Freeport area picked up quickly as a result. An attractive feature of Freeport property is that it is covered by the Hawksbill Creek agreement. Under this agreement, personal real estate is tax free until 2015. Entrepreneurs have invested heavily in tourism infrastructure on Eleuthera Island and the Abacos as well.

Apart from selling their wares, local women also provide services such as hair braiding to the tourists in the Bahamas.

BANKING

The other major service-oriented economic activity in the Bahamas is banking, which employs 25 percent of the labor force. The Bahamas has been a well-known international tax haven for about 50 years, and as a result, some of the world's wealthiest citizens have made their homes there. Among the country's attractions are its political stability, its generous tax laws (there is no tax in the Bahamas on income, profits, or inheritance), and the ease with which people can reinvest their money. Many foreign banks have been attracted to the Bahamas for the same reason; Bay Street in the center of downtown Nassau has one of the largest concentrations of international banks in the world, giving it the nickname Little Switzerland.

In December 2000, partly as a response to appearing on the Financial Action Task Force blacklist of Non-Cooperative Countries or Territories (NCCTs)— that is, countries perceived to be noncooperative in the global fight against money laundering and terrorist financing—the Bahamas enacted a legislative package to better regulate the financial sector. This included the

The National Bank of the Bahamas is responsible for monetary regulation and keeping the economy stable.

creation of the Financial Intelligence Unit and enforcement of "know your customer" rules. Other initiatives included the enactment of the Foundations Act in 2004 and the planned introduction of legislation to regulate private trust companies. Many international businesses have left the Bahamas in response to these new rules.

MANUFACTURING

In 1999 the small industrial sector of the Bahamas accounted for only about 5 percent of the nation's GDP and 5 percent of employment. Government infrastructure projects and private construction provide the main industrial activity. The only shipyard in the Bahamas is in Freeport, and it specializes in the repair of passenger and cruise ships. There is limited production of minerals. Sand is dredged off the banks and used for limestone and the production of commercial sand, which supply the local construction industry. There is also limited production of salt for export to the United States. Pharmaceutical company PFC Bahamas produces a small quantity of products for export, and the Bahamas Oil Refining Company (BORCO) has a refinery on the islands, but these are individual enterprises and do not represent any large industrial presence. There is a substantial brewing industry. Companies such as Bacardi distill rum and other spirits on the islands, while international breweries such as Commonwealth Brewery produce beers including the Heineken, Guinness, and Kalik brands. Bahamians proudly declare that their own locally produced rum is so flammable it has been banned on airplanes.

An oil refinery on Andros Island in the Bahamas.

AGRICULTURE AND FISHERIES

This conch farm in the Bahamas is the only conch farm in the world where Caribbean queen conchs are raised from veligers to adults.

Agriculture and fisheries together account for 5 percent of GDP. The Bahamas exports lobster and some fish but does not raise these items commercially. There is no large-scale agriculture, and most agricultural products are consumed domestically. The Bahamas imports more than $250 million in food each year, representing about 80 percent of its food consumption.

The government aims to expand food production to reduce imports and generate foreign exchange. It actively seeks foreign investment aimed at increasing agricultural exports, particularly specialty food items. The government officially lists beef and pork production and processing, fruits and nuts, dairy production, winter vegetables, and mariculture (shrimp farming) as the areas in which it wishes to encourage foreign investment.

TRADE

The Bahamas's main exports are mineral products and salt, animal products, rum, chemicals, fruit, and vegetables. Major imports are machinery and transport equipment, manufactured goods, chemicals, mineral fuels, food, and live animals. The country's most important trading partner is the United States. Other trading partners include Singapore, Spain, Poland, South Korea, Japan, Italy, Germany, Guatemala, Switzerland, and Venezuela. The Bahamas has an increasing trade deficit because its imports have a much greater value than its exports: In 2006, exports were $674 million compared with imports of $2.401 billion. The imbalance is caused partly by the need to import building materials for the construction boom.

The Bahamas is a member of the World Trade Organization (WTO) and the Caribbean Community (CARICOM), an organization of 15 Caribbean nations and dependencies. CARICOM's main purposes are to promote economic integration and cooperation among its members, to ensure that the benefits of integration are equitably shared, and to coordinate foreign policy.

SHIPPING

Since amendments were made to the Merchant Shipping Act in 1995, making the Bahamas a more attractive registry for shipowners, the country has become the number-one registry of cruise ships worldwide and the third-largest overall ship registry in the world, behind Panama and Liberia. Some 1,650 vessels are flying the aquamarine, gold, and black flag of the Bahamas.

The Bahamas Maritime Authority, a semigovernmental organization created in 1995, provides administrative services to shipowners. There is a busy cruise ship terminal in Nassau, and a container transshipment port opened in 1997 in Freeport.

TRANSPORTATION

The international airports are in Chub Cay, Rock Sound, Great Exuma Island, Freeport, and Nassau. Bahamasair, the national airline, provides flights to these airports from adjacent countries as well as domestic service to some 19 small airports or airstrips on the islands. Most people entering the Bahamas do so via Miami, Florida. The main seaports are Nassau on New Providence and Freeport on Grand Bahama.

Containers of cargo being unloaded at Freeport on Grand Bahama.

The major islands have a good system of roads. Driving is on the left side of the road, unlike in America and Continental Europe. Most of the major islands have a bus service, and minibuses called jitneys travel to the main settlements. Several people traveling in the same general direction often share taxis, which are plentiful. Taxis come in many shapes and sizes, from compact cars to minivans and even limousines.

As the Bahamas is an island nation, transportation by boat is important. Twice a week mail boats leave Potter's Cay Dock in Nassau and head toward the smaller Family Islands. Mail boats used to carry mail, but today their primary function in the Bahamas is to carry cargo, which can be anything from livestock to dry goods. Mail boats tend to be somewhat older boats and are often brightly painted to reflect the colorful influence of the island culture, making them a good choice for travelers interested in an authentic island experience. Other boat travel options include ferries and yachts, and visitors can even charter their own boats.

Small parabolic reflector antenae, as seen here, are used to relay telephone communication in the Bahamas.

There are more cell phones than native Bahami-ans—374,000 cellular phones for a population of 309,156 people.

TELECOMMUNICATION

The telecommunications system in the Bahamas is totally automatic and highly developed. The Bahamas Domestic Submarine Network links 14 of the islands and is designed to satisfy increasing demand for voice and broadband Internet services. There were 430 main telephone lines for every 1,000 people in the Bahamas as of 2008.

WORKING LIFE

Estimates place the total labor force in the Bahamas at about 181,900, but because many Bahamians on the Family Islands are self-employed fishers and farmers, this statistic may not accurately reflect the actual number of working Bahamians. Of those Bahamians who work for employers, 50 percent are in the tourism industry, while 10 percent work for the government in one way or another. An estimated 5 percent work in the agricultural sector, and another 5 percent in manufacturing. The remaining 30 percent of the population are employed in other sectors, mostly services. The unemployment rate was 7.6 percent as of 2008, while the public-sector minimum wage was $4.45 per hour.

For the majority of Bahamians who work in the tourism industry, working hours are irregular or on a shift basis; others enjoy normal business hours from Monday to Friday. Business offices do not open on Saturday, although most stores do. Nothing much is open on Sunday, as going to church takes precedence, followed by relaxing.

A lighthouse keeper adjusts the kerosene lamp inside a 6-foot- (2-m-) high Fresnel lens. Fresnel lenses are commonly used in lighthouses because they concentrate light.

ECONOMIC DIRECTION BEYOND 2008

The Bahamas is experiencing an economic downturn as a result of the worldwide economic recession. Tourism numbers dropped significantly during the last quarter of 2008, and approximately 1,000 tourism-sector employees were laid off between September 2008 and September 2009. The Bahamas is focusing on construction and other infrastructure projects in an effort to boost the economy and create employment. Goals include continued development of tourism properties through large-scale private-sector investment, increased Bahamian ownership of tourism businesses, redevelopment of the Grand Bahama economy following major hurricane losses in 2004, and expansion of the financial sector.

The Bahamas, unfortunately, is located between cocaine producers in South America and cocaine consumers in the United States. One of the main routes for drug smuggling is through the Caribbean, and the Bahamas is right on America's doorstep. However, the United States has acknowledged that there is no country in the Caribbean whose police and defense forces cooperate more closely in an effort to counter the flow of drugs than the Bahamas. The Bahamian government is determined that the country is not seen as a place conducive to the transit of drugs.

ENVIRONMENT

Boats mooring in a bay off Saint John's island
in the Bahamas as evening light streams in

THE BAHAMAS'S ENVIRONMENT

is its fortune, as its main industry is tourism, and the number of tourists who visit each year is more than four times the population of the islands. Tourists are attracted to the Bahamas because of its abundant wildlife and pristine beaches.

The Bahamas is home to some of the healthiest reef systems and greatest marine biodiversity in the Caribbean. Citizens, residents, and developers all have an opportunity and responsibility to play a critical role in preserving these resources.

The Bahamas is a signatory to the following environmental agreements: Bio-diversity, Climate Change, Climate Change–Kyoto Protocol, De-sertification, Endangered Species, Hazard-ous Wastes, Law of the Sea, Ozone Layer Protection, Ship Pollution, and Wetlands.

A school of gray snappers swimming over Sugar Wreck in the clear, blue Atlantic Ocean of the Bahamas.

ANIMALS IN THE BAHAMAS

The archipelago has only 13 native land mammal species, all of which are endangered. Twelve of the native land mammals are bats; the most common mammal in the Bahamas is the leaf-nosed bat. The other native terrestrial mammal is the hutia, a cat-size brown rodent akin to a guinea pig. Wild boars roam the backcountry of some of the larger islands. Feral cattle, donkeys, and horses, descendants of animals released after the demise of the salt industry, outnumber humans on the southern islands. The Bahamas has plenty of slithery and slimy things, including 44 species of reptiles. The country's symbol could well be the curly-tailed lizard, a critter found throughout most of the islands and easily spotted sunning on rocks, its tail coiled like a spring over its back. Humpback and blue whales are often sighted in the waters east of the islands. Atlantic bottle-nose dolphins frequent these waters, as do the less-often-seen spotted dolphins.

Before being rediscovered in 1966, the Bahamian hutia was believed to be extinct, for it was hunted for its meat and preyed upon extensively by the pets of the early settlers.

POLLUTION

Pollution continues to be one of the main challenges the Bahamas faces in maintaining its environment. A number of laws are in place to protect the environment, but given the sprawling nature of the islands, enforcement is a challenge. Problems associated with marine, coastal, air, and land pollution could have long-lasting negative impacts on the environment if left unchecked. Major causes of pollution in coastal areas of the Bahamas include leaks and spills of petrochemicals; run-offs from land pollutants, including fertilizers and pesticides used in agriculture and landscaping; run-off of sediment from coastal development; seepage of sewage from septic tanks; and the improper disposal of garbage such as cans, bottles, plastic bags, and other household waste.

DUMPING The indiscriminate dumping of plastic bags and other materials onto beaches and into the ocean has had and continues to have a devastating impact on marine life. Turtles and other creatures, for instance, mistake plastic bags for jellyfish. In addition the indiscriminate dumping of materials such as heavy metals and lead compounds contributes to toxic air pollutants that can be harmful to human beings. The dumping of automobiles and consumer goods such as refrigerators throughout the islands is contributing to land pollution.

AIR POLLUTION Another major source of pollution in the Bahamas is carbon monoxide emissions from cars, trucks, and buses. These emissions are higher when vehicles are not properly tuned. Carbon monoxide makes it difficult for body parts to get the oxygen necessary to function at their optimum. Overexposure to carbon monoxide can result in dizziness, fatigue, and headaches.

PESTICIDES The use of pesticides is also a major concern. In a marine environment, pesticides can kill important ecosystems and disrupt food webs. Pesticides can also present a number of health challenges to human beings, particularly if they enter freshwater systems and contaminate drinking water.

Sea turtles can sometimes mistake a plastic bag for jellyfish, eat it, and choke to death.

Apart from sustaining marine life, coral reefs also draw many divers from all over the world.

CORAL REEFS

The coral reefs provide Bahamians with food. The nooks and crannies found between the various reefs are safe houses for an abundance of marine life ranging from spiny lobsters to yellowtail snappers. Coral reefs also provide the Bahamas with storm security, which is priceless. The growth pattern of reefs is such that they put themselves at the mercy of an oncoming wave and are the first to take the brunt of the storm, thereby decreasing the size of the incoming surge. A third benefit of the reefs is their boost to the Bahamian economy, in that their beauty and the marine life they house attract tourists from all over the world.

Sadly, the reefs are under threat from a number of sources. Improper fishing methods are causing serious damage to the coral reefs and the animals that live there. Some fishermen use bleach and detergent to drive lobsters from their dens, but this has destroyed coral reefs and reduced lobsters numbers. Oil seriously damages the reefs by killing the coral polyps that create them. Run-off of fertilizers into the ocean leads to increased growth of algae that can overrun the corals. Algal and bacterial blooms resulting from these excess nutrients can cause fish to die in large numbers. Excessive sedimentation from coastal development projects that seep into the ecosystems also create havoc by smothering corals and damaging the creeks and wetlands that serve as nursery habitats for commercially important species of fish. Fish accounts for up to 60 percent of the animal protein consumed by people living in developing countries such as the Bahamas.

CONSERVATION LAWS AND POLICIES

The Bahamas has quite a number of conservation laws in place to protect its natural environment. For instance, spear fishing and explosive fishing are illegal, and fishing boats are not permitted to have poisonous substances such as bleach onboard. Companies or people found using chlorofluorocarbon (CFC) gases in air-conditioning systems, aerosol sprays, or refrigerants will be fined up to $10,000 or even imprisoned. However, Bahamas fisheries laws still allow the catching and slaughtering of certain turtles, even though the Bahamas is a party to CITES. The Bahamas Sea Turtle Conservation Group is lobbying the international community and the Bahamian government to legislate protection of the sea turtles, all species of which are threatened or endangered.

Pine forests, such as this one in the interior of Grand Bahama Island, are now being protected by the Bahamian forestry department.

CONSERVATION ORGANIZATIONS

The Bahamas has myriad conservation organizations, both governmental and nongovernmental, to protect the environment. The Department of Agriculture in the Bahamas is responsible for the conservation and enforcement of wildlife laws, such as stopping illegal trade in the Bahama parrot, which is a very popular pet worldwide. The forestry department of the Bahamas government manages what little is left of the Bahamian forests.

The Bahamas Reef Environment Educational Foundation (BREEF) was founded in 1993 by Sir Nicholas Nuttall to address growing concerns about the state of the Bahamas's marine environments. BREEF is a nonprofit organization dedicated to protecting the Bahamian marine environment through education.

Apart from converting waste to energy, Bahamians are also exploring the use of solar panels on South Andros Island for additional energy.

The Bahamas Environment, Science, and Technology (BEST) Commission was established in 1994 to better manage the difficult implementation of multilateral environment agreements. It also reviews all environmental impact assessments and environmental management plans for development projects carried out within the Bahamas.

The Bahamas National Trust came into being due to an effort to save the West Indian flamingo and to create the world's first land and sea park. Today it has evolved into a statutory, nonprofit, nongovernmental organization devoted to the conservation and management of the country's natural and historic resources.

WASTE TREATMENT AND DISPOSAL

The Bahamas, like most other developing countries, is grappling with a tremendous waste problem. The Bahamas produces 300,000 tons (272,155 metric tons) of waste annually, and a proposal to convert the waste to energy is looking very appealing, given skyrocketing oil prices and the fact that landfills in the Bahamas regularly catch fire because as waste decomposes, it produces large amounts of gas that burns uncontrollably beneath the surface if it is not collected or vented.

Waste-to-energy plants produce biodiesel, capture landfill gas, and convert solid waste to valuable energy. These plants in the Bahamas would reduce the reliance on costly fossil fuels and allow the country to protect its precious environment by getting the critical solid waste problem under control.

For the Bahamas, thermal conversion plants are recommended. Thermal conversion does not entail burning waste; instead the garbage is heated and the resulting gases captured. These gases are then used to drive a turbine to produce electricity. When what is left of the garbage is put in the plant a second time, it yields more gases; what remains is an inactive mass that can be used in block manufacturing or road building. Capture of heat from the energy production can be used for desalination or to create coolants for food storage.

With waste-to-energy conversion, garbage is viewed as a fuel, not a costly nuisance. The Bahamas Energy Corporation (BEC) is actively considering these plants, given that the economy of the Bahamas relies totally on fossil fuel imports—$1 billion of fossil fuels were imported in 2008 alone.

A green turtle swimming in the clear waters of the Bahamas.

ENDANGERED ANIMALS

GREEN TURTLE Green turtles get their characteristic color from the color of their body fat. They can be found throughout the world in all tropical and subtropical oceans. The carapace (hard top shell) is mottled light to dark brown and streaked with olive green. Adults can weigh 200 to 500 pounds (91 to 227 kg).

When laying her eggs, the female green turtle drags herself out of the sea and onto a nesting beach. Using her hind flippers as shovels, she scoops out a bottle-shape hole and lays about 100 white, leathery eggs that look like Ping-Pong balls. She covers the nest with sand and returns to the sea, paying no further attention to it and never seeing her young.

The sun's rays heat the beach, warming the turtle eggs buried in the sand. The eggs develop in the nest and are ready to hatch in about two months. Almost all must hatch at the same time, for they all must share the work of digging out from the nest. When the hatchlings are an inch or two below the surface of the beach they become quiet and wait for the surface temperature to drop, indicating nightfall. Under the protection of darkness the baby turtles burst out of the nest and rush to the water. Phosphorescence, a light given off by certain organisms living in the sea, creates a glow that directs the turtles toward the ocean. The hatchlings instinctively head for this "bright" horizon. Tragically, in settled areas, hatchlings are now attracted to the bright lights of highways, hotels, and parking lots and head away from the sea instead of toward it. Thousands of hatchlings are killed this way each year.

Green turtles are listed in Appendix I of CITES, meaning that they are near extinction or very endangered. Fewer than 500,000 green turtles may remain worldwide. Unfortunately green turtles can still be harvested in the Bahamas during open season (August 1—March 31). While all sea turtles have edible meat, the green turtle is favored as the source of the best turtle meat for human consumption. Turtle cartilage, or calipee, which is used in the manufacture of clear turtle soup, is obtained primarily from green turtles. Turtle oil, used in cosmetics, is also obtained primarily from green turtles.

ROCK IGUANA Rock iguanas are large lizards. The Bahamian species of rock iguanas are usually some shade of brown. Most are 2.5 to 3 feet (0.8 to 0.9 m) long. Young iguanas eat mostly plants and insects. Later in life they become almost complete herbivores (plant eaters), feeding on the leaves,

Rock iguanas resting on Great Exuma Island in the Bahamas.

fruits, and flowers of a large variety of plants including some, such as manchineel, that are toxic or noxious to humans. Rock iguanas thrive in dry areas where there are sandy patches for breeding, limestone that provides holes to retreat in, and shade to regulate body temperature. The Andros rock iguana is the largest iguana in the Bahamas and can grow to a length of 6 feet (1.8 m). It can also live up to 40 years.

All rock iguanas in the Bahamas are protected by the Wild Animals (Protection) Act. At present, the International Union for the Conservation of Nature (IUCN) lists all Bahamian populations of rock iguanas as "rare." CITES lists the rock iguana, like the green turtle, in Appendix I. All international trade is prohibited among CITES signatory nations. Subspecies of rock iguanas are found on Andros, San Salvador, Acklins, Mayaguana, and the Exuma Cays. On Andros, wild hogs, feral cats, and dogs are severe threats to iguanas. All other Bahamian rock iguanas are restricted to small, isolated islands where these animals do not pose a threat. Even so, there remains the continuous danger to all populations of iguanas of being harvested by man for food and the pet trade. In addition, natural disasters such as hurricanes are a constant threat.

A flamingo chick living peacefully in a conservation area in Great Inagua.

WEST INDIAN FLAMINGO The West Indian flamingo's long legs, long neck, characteristic pink color, and heavy, down-curved bill make it a bird unlike any other. The larvae of the salt marsh fly are a major element of the diet of West Indian flamingos. They also eat brine shrimp, small snails, and other forms of animal and vegetable life so minute that they can scarcely be seen without the aid of a microscope! Although small in size, this food is rich in carotene, the compound that gives flamingos their characteristic color.

In the 1950s it was thought that the West Indian flamingo might become extinct in the Bahamas because its numbers were so few and still declining. With the help of the National Audubon Society in the United States, the creation of the Bahamas National Trust, and the appointment of park wardens, the flamingo population of the Inaguas has grown to approximately 60,000—a true conservation success story. Even so, the West Indian flamingo is an endangered species. It is illegal to harm or capture this bird under the Bahamas Wild Bird (Protection) Act. CITES lists the West Indian flamingo in Appendix H, which means it is threatened and stands to become endangered.

NATIONAL PARKS AND RESERVES

The Bahamas National Parks system protects the world's largest breeding colony of West Indian flamingos, one of the world's longest underwater cave systems, a critically important sea turtle research facility, and one of the most successful marine fishery reserves in the Caribbean. In 2002 the park system was doubled in size, an unprecedented accomplishment in protected-area history. Ten new national parks were created, protecting both marine and terrestrial territories, bringing the total protected area under the system to more than 700,000 acres (283,280 ha).

The mangrove area in the eastern portion of Lucayan National Park on the island of Grand Bahama is home to a wide diversity of both plant and animal life.

HURRICANES IN THE BAHAMAS

The source of a hurricane's energy is derived from warmer-than-average ocean water along the equator and a corresponding higher level of humidity. In simplified terms, a low-pressure area is created when water-laden clouds release heavy rains as the warm air rises. Surface air spirals inward and upward in a counterclockwise direction to fill the partial vacuum, reaching tens of thousands of feet above sea level to become the hurricane's eye. While the eye is almost calm and is often exposed to blue sky, the winds nearest the eye are the strongest. More lives are claimed by storm surges and flooding than by the winds of a hurricane. A feature of global warming is that hurricanes in the Bahamas are increasing in intensity and frequency, bringing with them damage, destruction, and death.

HURRICANE WILMA, *which hit the Bahamas on October 24, 2005, caused $110 million worth of damage. It hit the Bahamas with winds of 186 miles per hour (300 km per hour) and flooded southwestern coastal areas of Grand Bahama. Power and telephone services were disrupted throughout the island. Four hundred structures sustained damage, of which about 200 commercial buildings were damaged so severely that engineers recommended they not be repaired.*

HURRICANE NOEL *in 2007 caused heavy rainfall across portions of the Bahamas, reaching a record 15 inches (380 mm) at one weather station. Sustained winds were around 40 miles per hour (64 km per hour) throughout the central and northwestern regions of the island chain. Extensive flooding was reported, especially on Great Abaco, forcing the evacuation of more than 700 people. Long Island was hit the worst, with floodwaters reportedly 5 feet (1.5 m) deep, which residents said was the highest they had been in 60 years. Roads throughout the Bahamas suffered damage.*

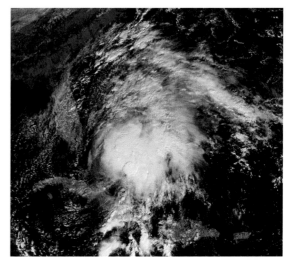

THE BAHAMIANS

A young Bahamian hesitantly investigates a cushion sea starfish off New Providence Island.

THERE ARE NO DESCENDANTS in the Bahamas of the first people to ever inhabit any of these islands; the Lucayans disappeared several centuries ago.

Many Bahamian families trace their ancestry back to the colonizing Eleutherian Adventurers who came with Captain William Sayle, seeking religious freedom by settling on the island of Eleuthera in 1647; to the Loyalists who migrated to the Bahamas after the Revolutionary War; and to the American Southerners who came just before and during the American Civil War.

About two-thirds of the population live on New Providence Island (where Nassau is located), and about half of the remaining one-third live on Grand Bahama (the home of Freeport).

Bahamians enjoying themselves on a boat. "True-true" Bahamians can be black or white.

All of these people brought their slaves, who eventually made up the majority of the Bahamian population. There are also Bahamians who claim as ancestors some of the more notorious pirates who made the Bahamas their home in the 17th century.

THE TRUE-TRUE BAHAMIAN

There are many definitions of what a "true-true" Bahamian is, but there is one thing that nearly all Bahamians have in common: No matter how they or their ancestors came to the Bahamas, they would not live anywhere else.

Interestingly enough, considering the racial divisiveness in many other parts of the world, ethnic origin is not a major issue in the Bahamas. Peaceful coexistence has been a way of life in the Bahamas for many generations, and racial conflict is very rare.

Local children enjoying a splashing good time at the sea.

AFRICAN BAHAMIANS

Approximately 85 percent of the Bahamian population are descended from migrants who came directly or indirectly from Africa. Many of them were slaves who migrated in the early 1800s, after the American Revolution, with their Loyalist owners to work the plantations on the islands. Unfortunately the plantations failed. Not long after, slavery was abolished, and the descendants of the former slaves stayed on in the Bahamas to become the backbone of its citizenry. Not all African Bahamians are descendants of slaves; some are descendants of freemen who were highly respected in their community.

Friendliness and warmth toward perfect strangers are characteristics of most African Bahamians. Above all, African Bahamians love a good conversation with nearly anyone and about nearly anything, although politics and sports tend to be favorite topics. It is not unusual to walk down the street in a Bahamian town, fall into earnest conversation with a total stranger, and become fast friends very quickly. By the same token, Bahamians are a very helpful people. If they see people who are clearly not local wandering around as though lost and in need of help, they will quickly overwhelm them with directions and advice—but first, they will probably want to know where these strangers came from, how they liked the Bahamas, and who their parents are.

The gregariousness of African Bahamians encompasses their large and extended families. Bahamian family gatherings, which take place during most public holidays, might well include grandparents, parents, children, and first, second, and even third and fourth cousins. Often all that is needed

San Salvador Islanders are likely to be descendants of former slaves left behind when Loyalist plantation owners migrated. The island's population is less than 500, more than half of whom live in Cockburn Town.

to be included in a family gathering is a common origin, such as having been born on the same island. Common interests, such as enjoyment of similar food and conversation, also give Bahamians the right to membership in a "family" group.

The disadvantage of this inclusiveness is that in any social circle everyone tends to know everyone else's business. Not that Bahamians are nosy, but they do like to gossip, and for this reason it is hard to keep secret anything that has the slightest tinge of scandal. The gossip is not usually malicious; plain curiosity is often the only motive.

"Laid-back" is another characteristic typical of many African Bahamians. This is rooted not in laziness but in an attitude that suggests there is no hurry— why rush to do today something that can well be put off until tomorrow or, better still, next week? It is all a matter of priorities, and many believe that enjoying life in the present is more important than the promise of the rewards that might accrue later through doing something "right now."

Due to the small comunities, local children share close-knit relationships.

CAUCASIAN BAHAMIANS

Caucasian Bahamians make up about 12 percent of the population. For the most part they or their ancestors came from Britain or the United States. Often they are better educated than their African counterparts, hold better jobs, and own finer houses. Today, however, this is not a cause of any tension. Bahamians have come a long way since the era of the Bay Street Boys, the Caucasian oligarchy of merchants and professionals.

A young Bahamian joyfully burying his father in the sand.

Caucasian Bahamians do have a different behavior and outlook from their black counterparts. Bahamians of British origin still tend to preserve their privacy by keeping very much to themselves, to a much greater extent than black Bahamians would ever think of doing. Caucasian American Bahamians are more outgoing, but they are equally unlikely to have strong personal friendships among the African Bahamian community.

CONCHY JOES

"Conchy Joe" is a slang term applied to anyone of Caucasian descent whose family has been in the Bahamas for as long as anyone can remember, even before the Loyalists arrived in 1783. Countless Conchy Joe families are now racially mixed, but the typical Conchy Joe is fair-skinned, with blue eyes and blonde hair.

THE "HAITIAN PROBLEM"

In the Bahamas, the expanding Haitian population is openly referred to as the "Haitian problem." There are currently an estimated 83,000 Haitians in the Bahamas; some are there legally, and others illegally. To native Bahamians, that is an intimidating 27 percent of the population.

Contrary to what many Bahamians think, however, the Haitians are not crowding them out of public schools and hospitals. While their low incomes force the Haitians to rely on government clinics and schools, statistics show that they make little use of social services and receive less than their fair share of National Insurance payouts.

About 8.8 percent of all schoolchildren are Haitians, the percentage of live births to Haitians in the Bahamas was about 11 percent in 2003, and in 2001 Haitians made less than 20 percent of all outpatient visits to public clinics—all numbers that are disproportionately low for the estimated size of the Haitian community. More than 12,000 registered Haitians contributed more than $3.5 million to National Insurance in 2004, but they received only 1.8 percent of total benefits, far less than might be expected from the estimated size of the population.

The Haitian community provides its own social services and has little contact with the government in this regard. And since many of the taxes in the Bahamas are indirect, they are paid by both legal and illegal residents. Given that the Bahamas badly needs the cheap labor the Haitians provide, many believe that the best thing the government can do is think about how to stabilize the size of the Haitian community and integrate long-term Haitian residents into the mainstream of Bahamian society.

Conchy Joes tend to stand out from both the African Bahamians and other Caucasian Bahamians through their enjoyment of ostentatious possessions and behavior. In fact, true Conchy Joes are proud to be part of the clan. Men who belong to this group are reputed to have a flattering manner with women, but they also to expect women to be conservative in their behavior.

HAITIANS

An increasing number of Haitian migrants now live in the Bahamas, particularly in the major cities, where they form much of the manual-labor force. Many Haitians came to the Bahamas as illegal workers, the majority having left Haiti in recent years to escape poverty and political repression. Haiti is one of the poorest of all Caribbean countries, while the Bahamas is the richest country in the Caribbean.

Haitians, who tend to be shorter and darker-skinned than most Bahamians, are mainly French Creole speakers and live in communities of their own, usually in the very poorest neighborhoods. Most members of this recent migrant population have not received much education. Both Caucasian and African Bahamians tend to look down on them, and some resent the Haitians for "stealing" jobs—even though most of these jobs (such as gardening, domestic work, and cleaning) are not ones that the Bahamians want for themselves.

A Creole girl on Long Island. Some Conchy Joes are also of mixed ethnic descent.

MINORITIES

Chinese, Hispanics, Greeks, and Jews make up about 3 percent of the population. Many of them arrived in the early 20th century from the United States, Hong Kong, and the surrounding islands. They tend to interact within their own communities rather than with other Bahamians.

BAHAMIAN DRESS

The proximity of the Bahamas to the United States means that American influence is very strong on the islands. There is little difference between the attitude to fashion in Miami and in Nassau, except perhaps for a certain island flair.

Chinese immigrants bring their culinary traditions with them, adding to the flavors of Bahamian cuisine.

Designer clothes are all the rage in the Bahamas, despite their high cost due to import taxes, and these are what Bahamians wear on the street—the flashier the better. Bahamians have a very exuberant color sense, and this is reflected in the combination of clothes they wear. They also apply their taste for vivid colors to their houses, which can be painted in every known shade.

As religion is a very important aspect of Bahamian life, most Bahamians possess an extensive Sunday wardrobe of church clothes. The hats worn by women are particularly important items of church attire, and proper shoes must be worn by all, with socks or stockings.

Many Bahamians also have a good knowledge of and interest in the ceremonial dress worn by their African ancestors, including the Ibo, Mandingo, Yoruba, and Congo tribes. They very rarely wear African-style clothing, however, except on very special occasions.

Hairstyles are important to Bahamians, especially the women. No amount of attention to grooming, braiding, perming, straightening, or tinting is too much if it means achieving just the right result.

PEOPLE-TO-PEOPLE

One of the best ways for visitors to get to know the Bahamas and Bahamians is through the government-sponsored People-to-People program. Through this program, run by the Ministry of Tourism, tourists and visiting businesspeople are matched by age, interests, and profession with Bahamian individuals or families and spend some time in their company during their stay on the islands. This contact can be as simple as having a meal together or as involved as spending several days learning about the country and its attractions. Because Bahamians tend to be friendly and outgoing, this opportunity to understand them in their own environment often results in long-term friendship. Currently more than 1,200 Bahamians participate in the People-to-People program.

As part of the program, the People-to-People coordinator organizes a monthly tea party hosted by the governor-general's wife at Government House, the residence of the governor-general. Related programs target foreign students studying in Bahamian colleges, pen pals, and the spouses of delegates attending conferences.

The Bahamian dress code is more formal than that of the United States. For instance, islanders feel insulted if visitors attend church in working clothes such as jeans.

Bahamian women in their Sunday best.

LIFESTYLE

Colorful resort homes by the beach on New Providence.

CHAPTER 7

AVING FUN IS AN INTEGRAL part of the Bahamian lifestyle, and just about everything Bahamians do, at work and at home, includes this element. Enjoying life in the present is often more important than trying to reach the top or making a lot of money.

Bahamian ladies enjoying tea and a good chat.

The rural settlement of United Estates near Cockburn Town on San Salvador.

One consequence is that there is very little sense of urgency in the Bahamas, and the general attitude about time reflects this. Although events that are scheduled to happen at a particular time usually do (store opening hours, for instance), other indicated times may be merely approximate, especially outside the major cities. Taking a dinner invitation for 7:30 P.M. literally, for example, could cause a guest to arrive at least an hour before the host is ready to receive anyone. When a mail boat captain announces that his boat will depart at 10 P.M., it probably will leave sometime that night when everything has been loaded, but the chances of its leaving exactly at 10 P.M. are extremely slight.

URBAN VERSUS RURAL

The Bahamian islands have varying settlement patterns and degrees of development. The infrastructure—roads, housing, and even golf courses—of any island usually depends on investment by development companies that reap profits from sales of houses and condominiums to foreigners and vacationers. San Salvador, for example, one of the Family Islands, enjoyed several periods of development: first in the 1930s, when the entrepreneur Harry Oakes built a hotel (it failed); then in the 1950s and 1960s, when the U.S. Navy (using the hotel building as a base) ran a submarine and missile tracking operation; then from the late 1970s onward, when home and leisure developers realized the potential of the island for residents and vacationers. A Club Med opened there in 1992.

About 89 percent of Bahamians live in urban areas, where the pace of life is a little faster than in the rural areas. In the countryside, including many of the Family Islands, the rhythm of life often proceeds at much the same pace as it always has—in harmony with the seasons and the hours of daylight and darkness. Whereas urban dwellers tend to live in orderly communities characterized by a logical system of addresses and some uniformity in housing styles, home to a rural Bahamian can mean almost anything from a newly constructed brick house to a tin shack, and these are not necessarily built along a named road. Bahamians are generally proud of where they live and of their community, often using it as part of their identity when describing themselves. They have no natural preference for town living, and many urban Bahamians confess to envying those who live less hectic lives on the less inhabited islands.

Unique little colorful huts with red and yellow roofs in Nassau remain bright and cheery, much like the Bahamian people themselves.

HOUSING

The majority of Bahamians live in small houses, but what they lack in size, they more than make up for in color. It is not unusual to see an orange house with a purple interior, for instance, or grand ornamentation inside and outside the house.

There are some architecturally outstanding homes in the Bahamas, particularly in Nassau and Freeport, many of them in quite exclusive residential districts. These houses were built in the characteristic "island" style, with covered porches, shaded balconies all around on both stories, sundecks or gables, shuttered windows, and several doors. The interiors are graciously decorated. Outdoors they typically have a lush garden, carefully landscaped and tended. In Loyalist settlements one still sees old mansions and houses in the New England style. Whatever the size, style, or color of their house, Bahamians are very house-proud and hospitable. An invitation to a meal or simply to "set awhile" and talk is not uncommon.

THE ROLE OF THE FAMILY

Bahamians have a strong, fundamental belief in the value of the family. Many Bahamians come from quite large families. This is especially true of the black Bahamian community, where extended families that include cousins many times removed support each other financially as well as in finding work and negotiating settlements whenever family differences threaten to disrupt the peace and stability of the group.

Bahamians have great respect for their elders. Grandfathers and grandmothers often continue to live with one of their children and are important influences in the raising of their grandchildren. It is more common than it used to be for both parents to work outside the home, making the role of the grandparents even more important.

A Bahamian family enjoying a day out at the beach.

The traditional roles of parents in a Western country are the norm in the Bahamas. The father is the head of the family and the disciplinarian, while the mother concerns herself more with the domestic needs of the family—cooking, housecleaning, doing laundry, and looking after the children's welfare—even if she also works outside the home. Grown children usually continue to live at home until they have completed their education and often until they marry.

BAHAMIAN WOMEN

In 2007 the Bahamian parliament had the highest representation of women of any parliamentary democracy in the world: 60 percent. Women in parliament in 2009 included the president of the Senate, Lynn Holowesko. While the government respects the rights of women, the constitution and the law discriminate against them. Unlike men, women cannot transmit Bahamian citizenship to foreign-born spouses. Where no will exists, possessions of the dead pass to the oldest living male relative. Happily, women in the Bahamas are generally free of economic discrimination, and the law provides for equal pay for equal work.

Violence against women is a serious problem. A private, government-aided crisis center runs a public awareness campaign on domestic violence, and a domestic court presides over family matters such as legal separation, maintenance payments, and court orders to protect women against abusive partners. Women's-rights groups have cited a general reluctance on the part of law enforcement authorities in the Bahamas to intervene in domestic disputes.

The government provides a toll-free hotline with trained counselors for each inhabited island. These volunteers counsel women suffering from abuse at home.

COMING INTO THE WORLD

Many Bahamians are staunch Christians, so the Bahamian life cycle tends to be dominated by the customs of the church. Baptists make up the largest Christian denomination, followed by Anglicans, Catholics, Methodists, and

Local women working in a jewelry shop in Nassau.

A wedding celebration held in Nassau.

Seventh-day Adventists. At the same time, the African heritage of many Bahamians is still evident. For instance, a new child will almost always be christened in a formal ceremony in church with all the family in attendance. Godparents are often appointed to look after the child's spiritual welfare in the years to come. Before then, however, a black cord is likely to have been tied around the newborn's wrist to guard against the entry of evil spirits into the unchristened body, and a Bible might have been placed at the head of the crib to strengthen this protection. A traditionally superstitious new mother also carefully avoids walking over "grave dirt," or it may take her a long time to recover from the effects of childbirth! In the Bahamas a christening is a good excuse for a party and a gathering with the extended family.

THE WEDDING

Weddings in the Bahamas have taken place under almost all imaginable circumstances. The knot can be tied in conventional fashion in a historic church, under palm trees on one of a few thousand deserted tropical islands, in a privately chartered yacht, or even underwater with scuba gear. The more exotic weddings, however, are for the tourists. At the marriage registrar's discretion, a couple need to be in the Bahamas for as little as three days before they can be married there, though in normal circumstances the period of residence is 15 days.

The true-true Bahamian is likely to be traditional. "Pomp and circumstance" best describes the Bahamian wedding. Money is almost no object for any Bahamian bride: This is her day, and everyone must be reminded of it. The designs of the bride's and bridesmaids' gowns are extremely important, and no effort is spared to make the bridal entourage as spectacular as

Song lyrics and myths are traditionally used to teach morals to Bahamian children. On these islands the children are raised with much love but are taught to be disciplined.

possible. During the ceremony, music plays an important part (as it does in all other Bahamian celebrations), and the wedding march will almost always be heard in a church. After the ceremony, the reception is as lavish as the bride's parents can afford, complete with music and entertainment, speeches, and the ritual throwing of the bridal bouquet into the crowd on the couple's departure.

THE FUNERAL

If a wedding is an important social event, a funeral is no less so. The death of a loved one is of course a sad occasion, but true-true Bahamians go out of their way to make the sendoff for relatives and friends memorable. Obituaries published in the newspapers describe the deceased in glowing terms and invite all acquaintances to pay their respects. They can attend the wake, an occasion for all who knew the deceased to gather and talk about his or her life, from time to time refreshing themselves with generous amounts of alcoholic beverages. Wakes often begin in the evening and last all night, ending with a service conducted in church. Then the coffin is carried in a procession to the cemetery, to the accompaniment of music, perhaps from a brass band. The usual form is an outward show of grief through tears and the singing of dirges.

Graves adorned with fresh flowers in Nassau.

EDUCATION

Up to the mid-19th century, education in the Bahamas was provided to the children of well-to-do white families and only selectively to academically able nonwhites, mainly through church-funded schools. Those who could afford an overseas education sent their children to schools in the United States, Canada, and Britain. Public education from the late 19th to the early 20th century was provided by Christian missionary schools.

Today school attendance is universal throughout the Bahamas. There are more than 200 schools, the majority of which are funded and run by the government through the Ministry of Education. They coexist with private schools founded by various religious orders.

The literacy rate in the Bahamas is approximately 95.6 percent, which rivals that of developed countries and is considerably higher than the rate in most third-world countries. Education is compulsory from ages five through 15. The Bahamian educational system is based on the traditional British model, in which students pass through various standards or levels: six years in primary school (ages 5—11), three years in junior high school (ages 11—14), two years in senior high school (ages 14—16), and two years in sixth form (ages 16—18), the equivalent of 11th and 12th grades in the American education system. Students take periodic proficiency examinations: the Bahamas Junior Certificate at the end of junior high, the General Certificate of Education (GCE) "O" (Ordinary) levels at the end of senior high, and the GCE "A" (Advanced) levels at the end of sixth form. The first two examinations cover a wide range of subjects from English and math to science, arts, and physical education; one school in the Bahamas offers a sixth-form course in science subjects leading to the GCE "A" levels.

Uniforms are the rule for schoolchildren in the Bahamas.

Bahamians take advantage of the good medical care provided by public hospitals and clinics, but at the same time many of them, especially on the Family Islands, retain a strong belief in folk medicine to cure common ailments, and even some less common ones. When used as a tea or in other liquid concoctions, cerasee (Mormodica charantia) is said to be effective against anything from the common cold to cancer. The traditional Bahamian believes that a poultice of pepper leaves reduces boils, dried goat droppings are effective against whooping cough, ground snails remove warts, and hog grease is a remedy for hair loss. Tea brewed from the leaves of a tree called the five-finger or chicken-toe is believed to relieve body aches. A salve of white sage leaves is applied to the skin to soothe chickenpox and measles. Wild guava is eaten by diabetics.

Of all the Family Islands, Cat Island is considered the stronghold of bush medicine, and many of the islanders there have the reputation of being effective healers. The island tradition in herbal remedies is included in the education program at the Rand Memorial Nature Center in Freeport, which displays exhibits and offers lectures on the subject.

There are several private adult vocational schools, as well as the College of the Bahamas (COB), established in 1974. The COB offers bachelor's degrees as well as two-year associate's degrees, with credits that can be transferred to affiliated colleges in Britain, Canada, and the United States; a further two years' study at one of these colleges leads to a bachelor's degree. The Bahamas is affiliated with the University of the West Indies (UWI), which has campuses in Barbados, Jamaica, and Trinidad.

HEALTH AND WELFARE

The government-run Bahamian health-care system covers the more populated islands. Nassau on New Providence has the largest public hospitals with state-of-the-art diagnostic equipment. Freeport on Grand Bahama has the government-run Rand Memorial Hospital. The other islands have clinics with resident doctors and nurses. Those who need specialist services not available in the Bahamas go to clinics in the United States, especially Florida, usually through a referral by their doctors. Many doctors who practice in the Bahamas trained in medical colleges in the United States, Canada, or Britain, or at the University of the West Indies.

A mandatory government-run insurance plan provides retirement, disability, medical, maternity, and funeral insurance. Premiums are deducted from workers' salaries, and employers also make contributions. The ratio of payments by worker and employer varies with the salary.

THE IMPORTANCE OF MIAMI

The northern islands of the Bahamas lie close to the coast of Florida; the nearest islands, the Biminis, are only 50 miles (80 km) away. Since the early 20th century, Americans have made the Biminis a vacation getaway, usually reaching the islands by yacht. The most famous of these is probably Ernest Hemingway, who described his experience in the Biminis in *Islands in the Stream*. It was published in 1970, after Hemingway's death.

In recent years, the traffic has been in both directions. Making frequent trips across the narrow strip of the Atlantic dividing the two countries is the goal of many Bahamians. They may travel for a short holiday, for medical treatment at a hospital or clinic, or to visit friends, but the usual reason is to shop from the much wider selection of goods available on the American mainland. Clothes, electronic equipment, and housing materials are particularly in demand, and Bahamians can often be seen at the airport in Miami loaded down with such purchases. Import taxes in the Bahamas are extremely high and duty-free allowances comparatively low, so shopping is not a pastime that most Bahamians can indulge in nearly as often as they would like, but it explains why there are airplanes leaving every hour from Nassau to Miami.

DO'S AND DON'TS

Bahamians are an extremely hospitable and friendly people. Whether on a Family Island or in Nassau, much of Bahamian life is lived outdoors, as the

Women chatting on Harbour Island.

climate is quite dry and warm most of the year. It is common to see household members doing chores, visiting with friends, or just resting on the front porch. It is sociable to be outdoors, ready to greet neighbors and passersby, and generally keep in touch with district affairs.

Showing respect to a casual acquaintance is important. The correct greeting is always appreciated. For example, identifying oneself clearly is important to a Bahamian; a stranger who fails to do so will most likely be asked where he or she comes from. Ignoring someone who is making friendly overtures is considered the height of bad form. Returning hospitality is important, from a verbal or written expression of gratitude to taking someone out for a meal.

Personal questions are the norm. Bahamians are by nature curious, and they like to know all about people they meet. Yet they are seldom intrusive, for they also sense others' need for privacy. Their friendliness sometimes encourages people to make the mistake of being too open about other people and gossiping. Bahamians do this all the time with each other in fun, but jokes and gossip are shared only within their own circle.

Eye contact is quite rare. Bahamians also strongly discourage staring, as they are at heart quite reserved and do not like being looked at aggressively.

Above all, Bahamians are a relaxed and easygoing people with an engaging sense of humor and an elastic sense of time—they call it BT, or Bahamian Time. They always welcome people to their homes and to their islands, just as long as visitors understand the rules and do not overstep the bounds of island propriety or custom.

RELIGION

The historical Mount Alvernia monastery on Cat Island. From these high cliffs comes a stunning view down to the densely forested island with its lovely and almost never-ending pink-and-white sand beaches.

THERE ARE VERY FEW BAHAMIANS who are not Christian. This is mainly due to the overwhelming number of the population descended from either British migrants or African slaves converted to Christianity by their original owners.

There are a few Muslims and even fewer Hindus, migrants who came to the Bahamas for work-related reasons, but they are dwarfed by both the size and the fervor of the Christian community.

Where in the world but in the Bahamas could people once fly with an airline called Trinity or buy real estate from a company called Put God First?

Beautiful stained glass adds shades of light into the Christ Church Cathedral in Nassau.

THE IMPORTANCE OF CHRISTIANITY

Christianity in its various forms is a very important part of the fabric of daily life in the Bahamas. For almost all Bahamians, going to church on Sunday is the rule, and many people keep a Bible handy in a drawer at home or at work to read in their spare moments. Religious celebrations, both national and personal, often include big processions and displays.

THE FAITHS OF THE BAHAMAS

Many denominations of the Christian faith can be found on the islands. Christian Bahamians may be Anglicans, Baptists, Church of God, Mormons, Nazarenes, Jehovah's Witnesses, Methodists, Seventh-day Adventists, Lutherans, or Roman Catholics. Churches run the gamut from almost cathedral-size to small single-room buildings. No community worth its name would be without at least one church even if, as on the smaller islands, the minister has to go island-hopping by mail boat to hold services.

Worshipers lean forward, kneeling in prayer at the East Street Tabernacle of the Church of God of Prophecy in Nassau.

The one thing that Bahamians of all these denominations have in common, beside their obvious acceptance of the Christian faith, is that religion is a very serious matter to them and an integral part of their daily lives. Another characteristic is that many Bahamians like to participate unrestrainedly in the services of their chosen church. For instance, many Bahamian churches offer "testimony services" that give worshippers a chance to repent publicly of past sins and to seek forgiveness from the congregation as a whole.

SUPERSTITIONS

There is no apparent conflict between Bahamians' strict adherence to the Christian faith and their strong belief in supernatural spirits' ability to affect human lives. Such folk beliefs have been handed down through the generations and go back to the African ancestry of many black Bahamians. They are still practiced to some degree by even the most educated.

The Bahamas has the highest ratio of churches per capita in the world.

If a Bahamian thinks he has become the victim of some malicious spirit, he may mark a series of *X*'s around himself and repeat the phrase "10, 10, the Bible, 10" to offset the bad influence. Someone who is seriously concerned about an evil influence may also sprinkle a particular kind of seed called guinea grain around the place to keep malicious spirits so occupied (they have to pick up the seeds one by one, counting them as they do so) that they will not have time to do their evil work. Love potions are popular: "Cuckoo soup" is a dark-colored broth believed to have tremendous powers; one sip and the victim is hooked, no matter what his or her feelings were toward the perpetrator.

The Greek Orthodox church in Nassau welcomes everybody with its soothing shade of purple blue.

On the darker side, there are still Bahamians who believe in the black arts of obeah, a kind of voodoo that they think confers special powers on the believer. Obeah is a blend of West African traditional practices and rituals with the beliefs (primarily Christian) that were taught to the African slaves by their European captors. Although obeah is officially banned in the Bahamas, it is still possible to find some people who practice it. Obeah practitioners are well known in the community and even advertise under titles such as "spiritual healer" and "psychic adviser." They believe in their ability to control the lives of other people under certain circumstances. Naturally shed parts of a person (hair, fingernails) or even dirty laundry are thought to be sufficient material for an obeah practitioner to put a spell or curse on a victim. The only remedy is to find someone with stronger powers to remove it.

There is both black (bad) and white (good) obeah magic. An example of white magic is a dream book: Traditionalists keep one in the belief that good spirits will help them find prosperity, perhaps through winning a lottery by transmitting the winning numbers to them in their dreams. The dream book is to write down what numbers come to them when they sleep.

Despite the high proportion of Christians in the population, since 1976 more than 60 percent of the children born in the Bahamas were born to mothers out of wedlock. According to the Bible, sex before (and outside of) marriage is forbidden.

LANGUAGE

Advertisement boards at a corner in Dunmore Town, on Harbour Island.

THE OFFICIAL LANGUAGE OF THE Bahamas is English, and anyone who speaks a variant of it as his national tongue can communicate in the Bahamas, even if street Bahamian English sounds like no other language in the world. There are actually two English language forms used in the Bahamas: "standard" Bahamian English and a Bahamian dialect with a structure that draws heavily on those of various African languages.

All the lessons in school are in English, as the education system is based on the British model.

The Bahamian dialect of English has the same musical rhythm one often hears among Caribbean islanders. True-true Bahamians speak both standard Bahamian English and the Bahamian dialect, crossing comfortably from one to the other. They usually know which one is more appropriate and apt for a particular situation.

There are also some French Creole speakers among the Haitian immigrants, but this language is very much confined to their own community, and very few true-true Bahamians understand, much less speak, this special form of the language.

TALKIN' BAHAMIAN

Standard Bahamian English follows the formal rules of British English—the Queen's English that is heard in Bahamian law courts, for example, or the English taught in schools. In those situations where standard English is appropriate, Bahamians speak with a distinctly British accent, as opposed to an American one, for example. What makes the Bahamian spoken dialect in daily use unique is that it disregards many Standard English rules. For

When kidding around, these young schoolgirls are likely to break into dialect.

Here are some popular Bahamian slang terms and their meanings:

- *big-eye — greedy*
- *biggety — brash*
- *bright — light skinned*
- *to buck up — to crash a car*
- *Conchy Joe — Bahamian of Caucasian descent*
- *cut hip — to give a beating*
- *duff — boiled, fruit-filled dough*
- *gussy-mae — fat Bahamian girl*
- *jack — friend*
- *to jook — to stab*
- *sip sip — gossip*
- *sweetheart — affair*
- *tree — three*

example, the use of tenses often focuses on the present regardless of the period of time concerned: "I gone to work yesterday" sums up the past, while "We see you tomorrow" takes care of the future. Similarly plurals are created simply by the context ("I have four nice dress"), and emphasis is provided through repetition ("That girl is pretty-pretty").

Bahamians also have some quite distinctive and unique words in their vocabulary, such as *boungy*, or buttocks, and *grabalishus*, which describes a greedy person. Some common English words show up in radically changed forms too. For instance it is quite possible in the Bahamas to catch *ammonia* (pneumonia) or even *browncurtis* (bronchitis).

Bahamian proverbs show a similar inventiveness of language. "It ain't for want of tongue that cow don't talk" means "Just because people have the ability to speak doesn't necessarily mean they always should." "The wind don't blow in the same dog tail all the time" means "Patience—your turn will come eventually."

The signs lead in every direction, and from Nassau to Andros, English is spoken, although sometimes with a different accent.

All of this is spoken with a special lilt in the voice, often with a rising inflection at the end of a sentence and the addition of the word *eh* at the end if a question is being asked—"She be coming today, eh?"

PRONUNCIATION Standard English speakers may have to depend on context to follow a conversation in Bahamian patois because in fast-paced dialogue, words lose their consonants, have their vowels changed, or are otherwise rearranged by a transposition of letters. For example, "them" becomes *dem*, "woman" *ooman*, "man" *mon*, "film" *flim*, "you" *yo*, "thought" *tot*, and "smash" *mash*. In addition endings are lost, so that "cleaning" becomes *cleanin'*, "don't" *dun*, and "child" *chile*. Those accustomed to Jamaican patois will have little trouble, since the Bahamian version is more recognizable to the standard English speaker than Jamaican.

NAMES, BABY!

Bahamians have elevated the invention of first names to a fine art, possibly because there are surprisingly few surnames around in the Bahamas. Many surnames go back to the British Eleutherian Adventurers or the white Loyalist settlers of the 17th and 18th centuries—for example, Albury, Higgs, Johnson, Smith, and Stubbs. Also, all the slaves belonging to one owner carried his surname.

The wide variety of unusual first names in modern Bahamas shows the creativity that goes into naming Bahamian children. This is done by choosing from a wide range of prefixes, combining these with a known name, and then sometimes adding a suffix as well, just for good measure. Other variables include adding the ethnic origin or the name of a film star or a royal personage. Royalty is a familiar theme, perhaps because the Bahamas was a favorite leisure spot with British royalty.

Female first names include the uncomplicated Sarah or Jeanne and the far more exotic Lashandra, Rayniska, Raymondessa, or even Marilyn Monroe. Male names could be anything from the biblical Abraham and John to Deshawn, Tameko, or even Prince Albert.

Satelite dishes, such as this one outside a house in the Bahamas, give locals a wide range of television programs.

KEEPIN' UP WIT' THE NEWS

Considering the widespread nature of the country, continuous access to the media plays a most important part in keeping Bahamians entertained and up to date about current events in the Bahamas and the rest of the world.

Radio Bahamas broadcasts throughout all the Bahamian islands nonstop via four stations, each offering different programming or focusing on a different geographic area. There are also two privately owned radio stations. On some islands, however, it is easier to tune in to Florida stations. There is also a television service by the Bahamas Broadcasting Corporation, which offers programming 24 hours a day, seven days a week. In addition, most Bahamians have access to a wide range of programs from the United States using satellite dishes or by subscribing to cable networks.

The Nassau *Guardian* and the *Tribune* are major newspapers published in Nassau and available on all the major islands. Two daily newspapers, the *Bahama Journal* and the *Freeport News*, are published in Freeport. But most Bahamians outside the major centers rely much more on broadcast news than they do on newspapers, for the news is old by the time newspapers arrive by mail boat at some of the more remote islands.

ARTS

Locally made masks and polished conch shells add
to the lovely array of colors seen in the Bahamas.

BAHAMIANS EXCEL IN THE performing and visual arts, and they like nothing better than having an excuse to display their talents. Musicality seems to come naturally to the average Bahamian. This, combined with a flair for unique uses of color and decoration in folk art and blended with both African and European traditions, leads to some unique expressions of Bahamian art.

The National Art Gallery in Nassau is home to the works of local artists.

Goombay drums,
used at the
Junkanoo and
goombay festivals,
have been traced
to West African
djembe drums.

MUSIC AND DANCE

Bahamians love to sing and dance and do both with tremendous enthusiasm. Songs are an intrinsic part of their oral tradition. Bahamian storytellers weave morals and myths into musical folktales. They call this musical improvisation ad-libbing, rigging, or chatting and use it not only for entertainment but also in church.

The annual Junkanoo parades are by far the most popular form of expression in music and dance, but their popularity has much to do with goombay music.

GOOMBAY On the islands the beat of goatskin drums accompanied by bongos, conch-shell horns, maracas, rattles, "click" sticks, flutes, bugles, whistles, and cowbells can be heard year-round in both impromptu and rehearsed performances. The different renditions of goombay are unique; the only common thread running through them all is a fast-paced, regular, and sustained melody.

Goombay music was imported a few centuries ago through the slave trade from the west coast of Africa. It is a mixture of rhythmic African drumming ("talking drums" were used to communicate over distances) and

A rake 'n' scape band playing in front of the beach in the Bahamas.

traditional slave songs developed during the many years of black oppression in North America. This percussion music was made famous by Alphonso "Blind Blake" Higgs, who played to tourists arriving at Nassau (now Lynden Pindling) International Airport for several years.

Today goombay music is commercially packaged in all the tourist hotels, where colorful, ruffle-sleeved dancers (usually male) gyrating to the goombay beat are the expected entertainment. As it is a part of the Junkanoo festival in December, people sometimes refer to it, incorrectly, as Junkanoo music. Every summer, beginning around June, the islands reverberate in a four-month-long goombay festival. One popular goombay artist was Tony McKay, also known as Exuma, the Obeah Man. Something of a cult figure, he was known for his outrageous costumes and long, braided hair.

RAKE 'N' SCRAPE Another kind of music found throughout the islands, usually played in bars and clubs and during festivals and regattas, is rake 'n' scrape. This is impromptu music played on accordions and guitars, usually accompanied by a variety of homemade instruments ranging from shakers made of seed-filled pods to saws played with household implements.

A guitarist captivates the attention of passersby with his simple but catchy tunes.

REGGAE, RAP, SOCA, CALYPSO, HIP-HOP, AND R&B are other rhythms that have emerged in the Bahamas in the past decade. They are often integrated with goombay sounds, but one usually has no problem identifying the different musical styles. Reggae and calypso are sounds associated with Jamaica, while soca is a Caribbean dance music with a pounding beat derived from calypso and American soul music.

SPIRITUALS and church music are close to the Bahamian soul. Attending church and participating in the choir are very important to Bahamians, so most churches have a well-developed choral music tradition. Spirituals brought to the Bahamas by slaves from North America feature predominantly.

Local art, with its bold brush strokes and vivid colors, keeps the cultural past of early Bahamians alive.

The Bahamas has a unique type of handicraft: coral and stone art featuring hand carvings, cultivated from naturally occurring reef breakoffs, beach erosions, and outcrops.

There are many variants of these, including the call-and-answer type of singing in which the choir and the congregation exchange questions and answers in song—this is the chatting or rigging that is part of Bahamian music.

The fire dance in the Bahamas has become a thing of the past, but before the 1940s, African Bahamians used to congregate at night by fires to sing and dance. Dances were often secret, as they were considered wild and unchristian. Fire dances did, however, become a tourist attraction, and there were several performances at hotels in the 1940s and 1950s.

LITERATURE

Recently a growing number of books have been written by Bahamians about the Bahamas. Among the best of these are several books by Patricia Glinton-Meicholas on Bahamian life and culture, especially *How to Be a True-True Bahamian* and *Talkin' Bahamian*. Although only partly about the Bahamas, the actor Sidney Poitier's autobiography, *This Life*, offers insights into life on Cat Island, where he was born and raised. Another Bahamian autobiography that islanders enjoy reading is Leonard Thompson's *I Wanted Wings*. Marion Bethel is a well-known Bahamian poet whose writing has appeared in American literary journals. She was awarded the Casa de las Americas Prize in 1994 for her book of poems, *Guanahani, My Love*. Today she lives in Nassau.

VISUAL ARTS

Only recently has there been a flourishing of indigenous Bahamian painting. Many contemporary Bahamian artists use the Bahamas as their inspiration, painting landscapes and seascapes, Bahamian houses, Junkanoo dancers and musicians, and other Bahamians in brightly colored settings. Some Bahamian artists are a little offbeat, such as Janine Antoni, who made headlines in 1993 when she lowered her naked body into a bathtub of animal fat! A leading Bahamian artist who has inspired young Bahamian artists is Amos Ferguson, whose primitive oils on cardboard carry four main themes: history, religion, nature, and folklore. Antonius Roberts is a Bahamian artist who is also an environmentalist. *The Last of the Casuarina Tree*, an art installation he assembled for an exhibition, has casuarina tree-trunk remnants and bottles of Kalik, a brand of Bahamian beer, filled with sand, letters, and editorials written in support of the casuarina trees that the government planned to remove from coastal areas in Nassau. (Traditional Bahamians hang Kalik bottles on tree branches as a protection against evil.)

HANDICRAFTS

Traditional handicrafts have always been a part of the Bahamian lifestyle. With increasing tourist arrivals, crafts have become an important local industry. Particularly at the Nassau Straw Market, visitors can find a wide range of products shipped there from other Bahamian islands. The most popular items are manufactured from natural materials such as straw dried from wild grasses. Straw products include bags, hats, baskets, dolls, place mats, floor mats, and other household items. Most of these are handmade, a simple sewing machine being the only mechanical equipment used.

Hardwood carvings and small pieces of furniture are popular as well. Local artists also make ceramic pottery. Tourists buy tumblers and figurines, some signed by famous artists such as Amos Ferguson, as souvenirs.

Souvenir straw baskets for sale at the Bahamian markets.

LEISURE

Lulled by the lapping of the gentle waves, this Bahamian woman relaxes in a comfortable hammock by the trees.

THE NEARLY PERFECT BAHAMIAN climate encourages people to spend much of their leisure time outdoors. With such easy access to the sea and lovely beaches close at hand, it is not surprising that many Bahamian leisure activities center around the water, although there are lots of attractions on land as well.

The sea provides ideal recreation for Bahamians and tourists, from sunbathing around hotel pools while enjoying the sea air to speedboat racing to enjoying the hues of pink during sunset on Andros Island.

Apart from the beaches along the shore, tourists also have the option of being in the middle of the ocean on a luxury cruise.

SWIMMING AND BEACHES

One of the most interesting facts about the Bahamas is that, although there is no official racial segregation, through custom and usage many of the country's major beaches tend to be used by either black or white Bahamians—but not by both at the same time. In the more populated islands, such as New Providence and Grand Bahama, major hotels monopolize many of the best beaches, with the result that these are used mostly by white Bahamians and tourists.

Most beaches in the Bahamas are pristine and unbelievably white, with sand so fine it feels soft to the touch. They are also often coupled with shallow transparent water for hundreds of yards out to sea, rising gently to sandbars before finally dropping into the depths. The hotel beaches are beautifully maintained, and many of them offer access to inshore coral reefs, enabling the more timid to enjoy the experience of snorkeling without having to venture too far into the water. Many black Bahamians go to the more secluded, less developed beaches. Simply sitting on the sand and "conversatin'" takes up as much of their time (or more) as actually being in the water.

Harbour Island is renowned for its pink-sand beaches. The pink color comes from shells and coral crushed by the waves over the years.

BOATING AND SAILING

Bahamian residents seem to prefer spending their time on top of the water rather than in it, so going boating in vessels of all shapes and sizes is quite popular. A sizable number of Bahamians own boats and use them for a variety of purposes, often chartering them out to the tourists for island touring or deep-sea sport fishing.

DIVING AND SNORKELING

The islands are a diving and snorkeling paradise. Many local companies cater to people who want to learn or practice either activity. It is easy to see the attraction of scuba diving for both locals and tourists, as the sea around the islands is full of exotic marine life and numerous old wrecks whose nooks and crannies make interesting places to explore. The water temperature remains constant year-round, which means it is possible to dive without a wet suit at any time. The underwater visibility is usually exceptionally good.

For those who would like to see the seabed but find scuba diving too adventurous, there is helmet diving. The helmet diver takes a walk along the seabed with a helmet on top of his head, into which is pumped a constant supply of fresh air from the diving boat. The diver's head stays dry, and he can wear contact lenses or adjust his glasses underwater. Each helmet dive lasts approximately a half-hour.

Besides viewing the large variety of marine life, scuba divers can also visit the Sugar Wreck found in the Bahamian Caribbean Sea.

College vacations see crowds of American students congregate at resorts in the Bahamas. Student group organizers set up stations, sometimes just a table and a few chairs outside their hotel, and dispense advice. They also keep a check on the behavior of members in their groups, for Bahamian authorities are on guard against undesirable behavior, especially in large groups of vacationing students. They like to maintain an image of the Bahamas as a desirable family resort destination.

There is no bad time to go, except that the southern islands may be uncomfortably warm in the summer, and one must be prepared for some wet weather in the winter. Loose-fitting cotton clothes, sandals, and protection from the sun—all easily packed into one carry-on bag—take care of personal effects for a week's fun by the sea, while those who prefer hiking need sturdier clothes and shoes for protection from thorny bushes and rocky limestone ground. Carousing does not end when the sun goes down, and student vacationers are generally well prepared for evenings of entertainment in some of the hotels that dot the beachfronts of the Bahamian islands.

Experienced scuba-diving enthusiasts like to try wall or cave diving, although neither is for the more cautious, as they often involve descents of more than 100 feet (30 m) in order to get into one of the underwater caves or blue holes. Snorkeling is a less dangerous pastime and requires only a mask, a breathing tube, and flippers. Swimming near the surface of one of the many Bahamian coral reefs, the snorkeler can see a colorful variety of marine life, ranging from moray eels and turtles to angelfish and parrot fish. For those who want to join in and swim with some of the bigger fish but are not prepared to scuba dive or snorkel on their own, a number of Bahamian companies offer experiences such as swimming with dolphins or even sharks.

FISHING

The Bahamas has the largest concentration of bonefish in the world.

Fishing is popular with both Bahamians and tourists. There are many possibilities, ranging from using a simple hook and line to working with all the complex gear of a deep-sea fishing expedition.

The bonefish is highly sought after in the Bahamas. These large-eyed, very bony fish can weigh from 5 to 10 pounds (2.3 to 4.5 kg) and be more than a foot (30 cm) long. They are challenging to catch, as they never stay in one place long and are extremely sensitive to sound. Bigger fish that provide sport for Bahamian fishermen include wahoo (many local tournaments are dedicated to catching wahoo), snapper, grouper, and marlin. Sport fishing is quite tightly regulated in Bahamian waters. Permits are needed for deep-sea fishing, and there are limits on how much fish can be caught by a single angler. There is no lack of charter boats to take enthusiasts to deeper waters to fish for sport fish such as the large blue marlin and tuna.

Christopher Brown is a Bahamian athlete who won gold medals in both the individual 400 m and the 4 x 400 m relay at the 2007 Pan American Games.

LAND SPORTS

The number of golf courses has increased dramatically during the past few years. It is now possible to play golf on most of the inhabited islands of the Bahamas, although New Providence and Grand Bahama have the most-prominent courses. Clubs organize tournaments regularly, and the Bahamas hosts leading international tournaments.

A saltwater fly fisherman holds up his trophy bonefish.

A family cycling along the beaches of the Bahamas.

In spite of the country's British heritage, cricket has become much less important in recent years than it used to be in the Bahamas and still is in many other former colonies. It used to be played fairly frequently, but since the 1970s it has given way to more American-oriented sports such as baseball, basketball, softball, and football.

HIKING, CYCLING, AND RIDING

The islands have coastal trails, and there are tracks running through many nature reserves, but the terrain inland is generally rough and overgrown with bushes. Hikers have to beware of sinkholes concealed beneath low bushes. Cycling and riding are less common on the islands, except at a few resorts that provide good roads for cyclists. Yet Grand Bahama hosts a 100-mile (161-km) road race for cycling enthusiasts every year, while an organization on Eleuthera organizes weeklong cycling trips. Mountain bikes fare better on the rough Bahamian terrain.

BIRD-WATCHING

The Bahamas is one of the world's best places to go bird-watching. There are numerous nature reserves dotted around the islands that are protected habitats for more than 5,000 bird species, one of the most spectacular being the Bahamian national bird, the pink flamingo.

CASINOS AND GAMBLING

A recently popular activity in the Bahamas is gambling in one of the several casinos that have sprung up on the more populated islands. To prevent the local economy from being devastated instead of enhanced by the advent of casinos, the government has enacted a law to prevent Bahamian residents from gambling in the casinos; gambling there is strictly for foreigners. Bahamians enter casinos for other entertainment or to work.

TRADITIONAL PASTIMES

Traditional games such as *warri* (WAR-ee) are part of the African heritage of the majority of Bahamians. Dominoes, checkers, and many varieties of card games are also still popular. Storytelling is an important part of the Bahamian leisure tradition. The telling of tales of magic and supernatural heroes has died out, but tales based on family history and local events, especially tales of disaster, are commonplace and appreciated by both young and old.

Players try their luck at these slot machines in the Atlantis resort and casino in Nassau.

FESTIVALS

An elaborate Junkanoo float during the Boxing Day celebrations. Prizes are given for the best Junkanoo costumes, motivating participants to create as distinctive a mask or float as possible.

Lead Cos
A-11
xing Day

BAHAMIAN FESTIVALS are lavish, long-lasting, and loud. Most of them tie in with Christian festivals, and some are expressions of national pride. But none exemplify the Bahamian spirit better than the Christmas and New Year's festival no true-true Bahamian would miss: Junkanoo.

A marching band plays during the New Year Junkanoo festival in Nassau.

Johnny Canoe, the folk hero who inspired Junkanoo, was an 18th-century African prince and slave trader on the Gold Coast who was successful in defending Fort Brandenbury from the Dutch for nearly 15 years. He was eventually enslaved himself and brought to the West Indies, but even as a slave he remained a leader of his people.

Children dressed as U.S. patriots during a parade.

JUNKANOO

No one knows for certain how this festival got its name, although some have suggested that it was named after Johnny Canoe, an African folk hero and tribal chief who demanded the right to celebrate with his people even after being made a slave. Many other people think the name came from the French phrase *gens inconnus*, meaning alien or unknown people. If this is true, it is appropriate for this festival because participants in a Junkanoo parade are masked to conceal their identity, similar to what happens during the celebration of Mardi Gras in the United States.

Participants dress up in a dazzling variety of colorful costumes, known as scrap, complete with hats and masks representing mythical and imaginary characters. They parade down the length of Bay Street in Nassau (the biggest Junkanoo parade in the Bahamas) and the main streets of smaller towns to the accompaniment of goombay music made with goatskin drums, gourds, cowbells, conches, horns, and whistles. The crowds lining the streets join in with or without instruments, imitating the *ka-lik ka-lik* sound of the cowbells. The object is to be as flamboyant and to make as much noise as possible.

Preparations for Junkanoo begin up to a year before the first "rush," as each parade is known, and are often very elaborate. Most of the participants belong to one of the many competing groups sanctioned by the national Junkanoo committee, which awards prizes for the best costumes and music. These groups—which can sometimes number up to 500 members and which give themselves names such as Saxons, Pigs, Valley Boys, and Music Makers—usually decide well in advance on a theme that will be reflected in the costumes of their members. The exact details of what everyone will be wearing and what they will represent are closely guarded secrets until they assemble for the parade.

Individuals can also take part in the Junkanoo procession, and their costumes are every bit as fanciful as the group ones though usually not as elaborate. There are minimum requirements for costumes in a Junkanoo parade, but usually the more colorful and fantastic the better.

Each of the major Junkanoo groups depend on corporate sponsors. A typical group requires anything from $40,000 to $100,000 to produce a winning formula.

Individual participants can also look forward to displaying their artistic creations.

Cardboard and crepe paper are common construction materials for the Junkanoo costumes, and paint and "tricks"—beads, satin, and plastic jewels among them—are used to embellish them. Because of the fragile nature of such materials, however, and the exuberance with which their wearers move about during the parade itself, many costumes do not survive the parade in very good condition. Fortunately the best of them have been preserved by collectors, and many are on display in the National Junkanoo Museum, a recent feature of the Nassau waterfront.

The first parade begins at 3 or 4 A.M. on Boxing Day, the day after Christmas, with streetlights shining on a sea of strange and wonderful characters. During the parade, participants stop and perform their dances at designated places along the route, while the drummers show off their amazing skill. This is called a breakout. When the parade continues, spectators join in, dancing to the music behind the performers. When the dancing ends, people gather for the prize-giving, after which the celebration draws to a close at about dawn. People straggle home exhausted, to recoup their energy for the second rush, on New Year's Day.

Even little children participate in the Junkanoo parades.

THE GOOMBAY SUMMER FESTIVAL

There are many reflections of the Junkanoo experience at other times of year besides December and January. One of the hotels even sponsors a mini Junkanoo procession every Friday night. Nothing comes close to the actual winter celebration, but one of the best replicas is the summer goombay festival, which combines the exuberance of a Junkanoo procession with goombay music performances.

REGATTAS AND OTHER MAJOR EVENTS

Whatever the time of year, some major party is happening on one of the islands. Chances are this will be a regatta, where the main show is a boat race, while sideshows such as beauty pageants and cooking demonstrations are enjoyed by noncompetitors. Other events include pineapple festivals, conch-cracking contests, and historical weekends to celebrate Loyalist roots. In all of these, music and food are always prominently featured.

Goombay dancers are usually male, but hotel shows featuring goombay music often employ dancers of both genders.

Goombay is said to be derived from the African word *nkumbi*. In the Bantu language, it describes a type of ceremonial drum.

The Royal Bahamas Police Band performing in front of a crowd during Independence Day, July 10. Two other national holidays are Emancipation Day (first Monday in August) and National Heroes' Day (October 12). The first celebrates the emancipation of the slave ancestors of the majority of Bahamians. while the second honors those who contributed to the history of the Bahamas.

NATIONAL HOLIDAYS

Among the public holidays are Bahamian Independence Day and Emancipation Day. Independence Day is on July 10, but the celebration lasts a week, with speeches, parades, and fireworks. Emancipation Day, observed on the first Monday in August, celebrates the anniversary of the freeing of slaves throughout the British colonies. In Nassau the end of slavery is also celebrated during Fox Hill Day, which takes place on the second Tuesday in August. Fox Hill Day owes its origin to the fact that it took about 10 days for news of freedom from slavery to reach the then somewhat isolated community of Fox Hill.

Another Bahamian holiday was Discovery Day, October 12, which commemorated the landing of Christopher Columbus on the island of San Salvador in 1492. Discovery Day was renamed National Heroes' Day in 2002, to honor outstanding people who made contributions that altered the course of Bahamian history or gave service to the Bahamas. Among the people honored during the first National Heroes' Day were Sir Lynden Oscar Pindling, the "father of the nation," who was the chief architect of the modern-day Bahamas, and Dame Doris Johnson, the first woman to run for parliament, the first female senator, the first female minister in government, and the first female leader of the Senate.

Easter is celebrated in Nassau with parties and Easter egg hunts. The holiday weekend includes Good Friday and Easter Monday. Whit Monday is celebrated seven weeks after Easter, a movable feast day that depends on the date of Easter.

On November 5, bonfires are seen everywhere in celebration of Guy Fawkes Day. This British import has nothing to do with the Bahamas (it is not even a national holiday), but the fun-loving Bahamians think it a good excuse to party! The instigator of the 1605 Gunpowder Plot to blow up the British Parliament is burnt as an effigy, and his death is further commemorated by extravagant displays of fireworks.

Public holidays are also occasions for extended Bahamian families to gather for a special homecoming celebration, with feasts, parties, songs, and long sessions of storytelling.

A limbo dancing party in the Bahamas. Parties go into full swing during the public holidays in the Bahamas.

FOOD

Fresh juices are readily available all over the Bahamas.

13

MANY DAILY ACTIVITIES in the Bahamas are conducted around the dining table or with a plate of one of the local delicacies close at hand. The contents of a meal and the sophistication of the dishes can differ from island to island, but the portions are always substantial. Due to the influence of the many races of people who have lived in the Bahamas during the past 500 years, the cuisine is quite varied.

The long-gone Lucayans' diet was predominantly seafood. This was supplemented with cassava, corn, and sweet potatoes, all of which are native to the Bahamas. British meat pies and roasts followed in their wake, but North American cuisine has taken over in popularity. The African influence is present in grits, johnnycakes, and peas 'n' rice, as well as in the flavorings. Bahamian flavoring ingredients include salt, nutmeg, ginger, chili peppers, lime, parsley, thyme, and tarragon.

CONCH

Although seafood in general plays a big part in the modern Bahamian diet, none is more common or more universally enjoyed than the conch. Conch is a snaillike mollusk found all over the Bahamas, and its white,

CONCH CRISIS

Overfishing has caused a drastic decline in the supply of conch throughout the Caribbean. During the past few decades, intense fishing pressure has led to the collapse of the conch fishery in many Caribbean countries. In the Bahamas the conch fishery is slowly getting depleted. Fishermen have to go farther to find conch, as the near-shore supply is drying up. In the Bahamas it is illegal to catch immature conch, but a large proportion of the conch catch are juvenile conch that have not had a chance to reproduce. In some parts of the northern Bahamas up to 90 percent of the conch landed are juveniles. Students in South Eleuthera studied old and new piles of conch shells. They found that in the piles at least 10 years old, 5 percent of the conch were juveniles, while of the conch caught today, 95 percent are juveniles. Catching conch before they have reproduced threatens the sustainability of this resource and the livelihoods of the fishermen who depend on it. The conch is listed as a threatened species by CITES. To reverse this, stronger enforcement of the Bahamian laws regarding harvesting conch is needed, and a network of marine reserves where no conch fishing is allowed must be put in place as quickly as possible, to allow conch to breed and the population to recover.

pink-fringed meat forms the basis of many dishes. It can be fried, grilled, steamed, stewed, or made into a raw conch salad, the conch meat diced and mixed with chopped onion, tomato, cucumber, and celery, then liberally sprinkled with pepper and lime juice.

After a first taste, a newcomer might wonder why a not particularly appetizing meat is eaten by Bahamians in so many ways—from gourmet dishes in fancy restaurants to conch fritters called cracked conch sold at small stalls on sidewalks. There are two reasons: Conch is cheap, and more important, Bahamians believe it to be a potent aphrodisiac.

In Bahamas a conch cracking contest is held on National Heroes' Day. Conch cracking requires dexterity in removing the meat: The cracker first hits the shell with a heavy implement to break it (it must be hit in the right spot, where the meat is attached to the shell), then "jewks" the conch out of its shell by grasping an appendage (commonly called a foot or a claw) and pulling it.

OTHER SEAFOOD

Crawfish (the Bahamian version of lobster) is also very popular, as is the land crab, which can be seen running around on many of the islands and is easily caught. It is often served stuffed with other food. From among the large variety of fish caught off the Bahamian coasts, grouper, a mild-flavored whitefish, is a particular favorite. This is often served with a spicy Creole-style sauce, followed closely by baked bonefish with a hot pepper sauce. Outside the more populated centers, many other varieties of seafood find their way to the table—turtle dishes are popular on the Exumas, for instance, while in other areas recipes can feature such marine life as yellowtail, snapper, grunt, jack, and even goggle-eye.

One of the most common ways of preparing fish, especially for breakfast, is "boil fish" or "stew fish," a kind of stew in which a firm-fleshed fish (often grouper) is put in the pot with salt pork, onions, potatoes, celery, tomatoes, and seasonings and then boiled until the appetizing aroma is sufficiently strong to tempt the cook to tuck into sizable helpings of the end result.

GRITS, PEAS, AND JOHNNYCAKE

Seafood and other meats are often eaten with side dishes, including some of the most traditional of all Afro-Bahamian foods: grits, peas 'n' rice, and johnnycake. All three are quite similar in appearance to dishes eaten in the southern United States, and indeed many of these recipes came over from the American South with the slave ancestors of today's Bahamians.

A generous mound of grits, ground cornmeal mush, with vegetables added often forms the basis of a meal. There are as many recipes for peas 'n' rice as there are people, for they depend on the individual blending of ingredients, the cooking time, and the sauces poured over them. Ingredients can range from simply pigeon peas (not green peas) and rice to pigeon peas and rice with salt pork, tomatoes, thyme, green pepper, celery, or virtually any other ingredients an inspired cook might choose to add. As for seasonings, individual taste dictates what these should be, common ones being salt, whole peppercorns, allspice, chili peppers, and chopped onions.

Rice cooked with pigeon peas and peppers, called peas 'n' rice, with a generous portion of papaya for dessert.

Johnnycake, once considered a poor man's food because it was the staple diet of impoverished early settlers, is a pan-baked bread made with milk, butter, flour, sugar, salt, and baking powder. Sometimes it is even baked in a sand-filled box on fishing boats. Johnnycake tastes rather bland, but it certainly fills the stomach.

SOUSE

A popular dish in the Bahamas, especially on the weekend, is souse. It is popular because of its ability to fill an empty stomach while requiring very little work from the cook. The meat ingredients can be anything: parts of a sheep, including the tongue; parts of a pig, including the trotters; chicken; conch. These are tossed into a large pot of salted water and boiled with spices and other ingredients. When the meat is tender enough to eat, it is ladled onto plates, liberally sprinkled with lime juice and pepper, and eaten with bread.

There are different kinds of souse. In England the meat parts (trotters and ears, for instance) are pickled in vinegar. In the Bahamas, however, spices are used in the cooking, and lime juice is added when serving to give it a sour flavor.

Cookouts are a favorite Bahamian social gathering. A typical serving of barbecued meat usually comes with potato salad, conch salad or fritters, coleslaw, and macaroni.

GUAVA DUFF

Dessert is as substantial as the main course, and none more so than the absolute favorite, guava duff. A duff is a boiled pudding filled with fruit (usually guava, but it could be melon, pineapple, papaya, or mango) that has a cakelike consistency and is eaten with a sauce. Good Bahamian cooks have their own recipe, often handed down for generations and jealously guarded. A good guava duff is time-consuming to make.

TROPICAL FRUIT

Many varieties of locally grown fruit are eaten raw or form the basis of desserts and drinks. Some of these, such as bananas, papayas, pineapples, and mangoes, are also popular outside the Bahamas. Others, including soursops, sugar apples, sapodillas, and jujubes, have flavors that may take a little time to appreciate. The dark green, irregularly shaped soursop is covered with soft spines and weighs from 1 to 5 pounds (0.5 to 2.3 kg). Its fibrous white pulp is refreshing; far from being sour, it is usually sweet with only a slightly tart flavor. The sugar apple belongs to the same family as the soursop. It looks like a green (sometimes purplish brown) pinecone about the size of a tennis ball. To eat it, one splits the soft fruit open by hand and spoons out its sweet, smooth, segmented white flesh, separating it from the shiny black seeds. The sapodilla is an oval, brown fruit about 2 to 3 inches (5 to 8 cm) across, with three to six black seeds. The flesh, which is pale brown and smooth but sometimes slightly grainy, has been likened to that of pear flavored with brown sugar.

Fruit of the Bahamas include bananas, sugar apples, and coconut.

DRINKS

Drinks in the Bahamas tend to fall into two categories: those concocted for and served mainly to the tourists who frequent casino resorts and those consumed by the locals. Those in the first category are based on varieties of rum and include such exotic concoctions as the Bahama Mama (rum, bitters, crème de cassis, grenadine, nutmeg, and citrus juices), the Goombay Smash (coconut rum, light rum, and mixed-fruit punch), and the Yellow Bird (rum, crème de banana liqueur, Galliano, and apricot brandy mixed with orange and pineapple juices). Drunk in quantity, the cumulative effect of these deceptively smooth-tasting concoctions can soon be quite lethal!

Nassau Royale is a locally produced liqueur that is included in some of the more exotic concoctions, but drunk by itself, it has a very pleasant rum-based taste. Some Bahamians prefer to stick to less exotic fare. They drink their rum straight or with water and find Kalik, the locally produced lager-style beer, very refreshing on a hot day.

For nonalcoholic drinks, Bahamians prefer those that are typically refreshing in hot climates—fresh lime coolers, for instance, and the more traditional sodas such as cola and ginger ale. Fruit juices are quite popular also, as is bottled water, since the tap water is a little salty. Coffee and tea are popular too, but perhaps due to the British heritage of the Bahamas, tea is often much better prepared than coffee.

The sugar apple is high in calories and a good source of iron.

JOHNNYCAKE

10 servings

2 cups (500 ml) flour

2 tablespoons (30 ml) baking powder

4 ounces (110 grams) sugar

¼ ounce (5 grams) salt

Pinch of nutmeg

4 ounces (110 grams) butter

1 cup (250 ml) buttermilk

1 egg, beaten

- Preheat oven to 400° F (250° C).
- Grease an 8-inch (20-cm) square pan with vegetable oil.
- Sift the dry ingredients (flour, baking powder, sugar, salt, and nutmeg) and form a well.
- Rub the butter into the mixture; add buttermilk and egg.
- Knead well, then put into prepared pan.
- Allow to rest for 30 minutes, then bake for 25—30 minutes.
- Cut into 2-inch (5-cm) squares and serve.

GUAVA DUFF

8 servings

¼ cup (60 ml) butter or margarine

1 cup (250 ml)sugar

3 eggs, beaten

2 cups (500 ml) guava pulp (guava put through a sieve or food mill)

½ teaspoon (2.5 ml) nutmeg

½ teaspoon (2.5 ml) cinnamon

3 cups (750 ml) flour

2 teaspoons (10 ml) baking powder

- Cream butter or margarine with sugar.
- Add eggs, guava, and spices, then beat until smooth.
- Sift together flour and baking powder and add to guava mixture; the dough will be stiff.
- Place mixture in greased top of double boiler and cook over boiling water for three hours.
- Slice and serve with butter-egg sauce.

Butter-Egg Sauce

4 tablespoons butter or margarine

¾ cup sugar

1 egg, separated

- Cream butter or margarine and sugar; add egg yolk and blend.
- Beat the egg white until stiff, then fold into mixture.
- If the mixture is too thick, a very small amount of hot water can be added.
- Serve over hot guava duff.

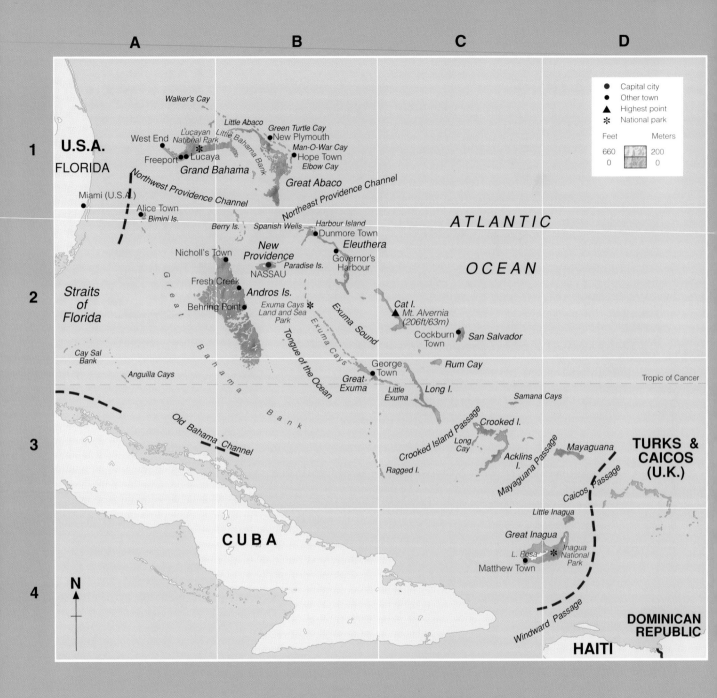

MAP OF BAHAMAS

ECONOMIC BAHAMAS

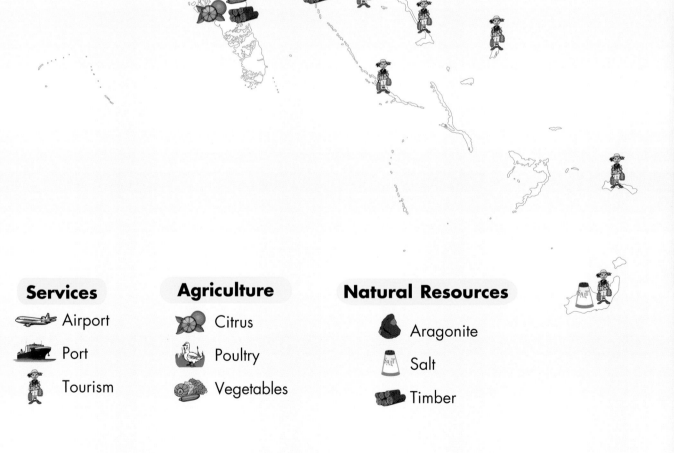

Services	Agriculture	Natural Resources
✈ Airport	🍊 Citrus	🪨 Aragonite
🚢 Port	🦆 Poultry	🧂 Salt
🧳 Tourism	🥬 Vegetables	🪵 Timber

ABOUT THE ECONOMY

OVERVIEW

The Bahamas is one of the wealthiest Caribbean countries, with an economy heavily dependent on tourism and offshore banking. Tourism together with tourism-driven construction and manufacturing accounts for approximately 60 percent of GDP and directly or indirectly employs half of the country's labor force. Steady growth in tourism receipts and a boom in the construction of hotels, resorts, and residences led to solid GDP growth in recent years, but tourist arrivals have been on the decline since 2006 and dropped even further in 2009. To help offset the effect of the global economic downturn, particularly on employment, the Ingraham administration plans to engage in infrastructure projects. Financial services constitute the second most important sector of the Bahamian economy and, combined with business services, account for about 36 percent of GDP. Manufacturing and agriculture combined contribute approximately 10 percent of GDP and show little growth, despite government incentives aimed at those sectors.

CURRENCY

$1 = 1 Bahamian $ (2010 estimate)
The U.S. dollar is maintained on par with the Bahamian dollar by the Central Bank of the Bahamas.

GROSS DOMESTIC PRODUCT (GDP)
$9.352 billion (2008 estimate)

GDP PER CAPITA
$29,800 (2009 estimate)

INFLATION RATE
2.4 percent (2007 estimate)

LABOR FORCE
175,500 (2007 estimate)

UNEMPLOYMENT RATE
7.6 percent (2006 estimate)

AGRICULTURE
Citrus and vegetables

NATURAL RESOURCES
Salt, aragonite, timber

MAIN INDUSTRIES
Tourism, banking, cement, oil, salt, rum, aragonite, pharmaceuticals, spiral-welded steel pipe, and transshipment

MAIN EXPORTS
Mineral products and salt, animal products, rum, chemicals, fruit, and vegetables

MAIN IMPORTS
Machinery and transportation equipment, chemicals, manufactured goods, mineral fuels, food, and live animals

MAIN TRADE PARTNERS
United States, Singapore, Spain, Poland, South Korea, Japan, Italy, Germany, Guatemala, Switzerland, Venezuela

CULTURAL BAHAMAS

Peterson Cay National Park
Peterson Cay National Park is one mile offshore of Grand Bahama Island. This small (1.609 km), often deserted island is a relaxing place for snorkeling and viewing birds. On the northeast of the cay is a lovely coral garden.

Lucayan National Park
Lucayan National Park on Grand Bahama Island has nature trails and boardwalks that lead to a variety of ecosystems. Within the park is one of the largest underwater cave systems in the world and two large caves.

Garden of the Groves
The Garden of the Groves on Grand Bahama has more than 10,000 species of flowers, shrubs, trees, and exotic plant life. The garden attracts many birds and butterflies. Along its shaded, winding paths are several waterfalls.

Hope Town Lighthouse
This lighthouse on Elbow Cay just off Great Abaco Island is one of the few remaining lighthouses in the Caribbean that is man-operated. The lighthouse offers a breathtaking view of the outlying Parrot Cay and Elbow Cay's enclosed harbor.

Devil's Backbone
The Devil's Backbone is a reef that runs parallel to the beach at Harbour Island. Scattered around the Devil's Backbone is an unbelievable collection of shipwrecks. The reef also has an amazing diversity of underwater life.

Preacher's Cave
The Preacher's Cave was used as a church by the early European settlers to Eleuthera who were shipwrecked on the Devil's Backbone. Artifacts from the 17th century have been found in the cave. Outside the cave is a beautiful pink-sand beach.

Nassau
Nassau is the capital of the Bahamas, and it has retained much of its older architecture and blended it with modern buildings. It is home to the Ardastra Gardens; Zoo and Conservation Center; Parliament Square; the famous Straw Market, and numerous other places of interest.

Watling's Castle
In the 17th century British pirate Captain George Watling took over San Salvador Island and made it his headquarters. This old pirate palace is now a visitor attraction where visitors can see the ruins of the house and slave quarters as well as beautiful views.

Hamilton's Cave
Hamilton's Cave on Long Island has artifacts and prehistoric cave drawings from the Lucayan tribe, the first known settlers in the Bahamas. Visitors can explore the ancient cave system, view historical cavern drawings, and see the remains and relics of the early history of the Bahamas.

Mount Alvernia
Mount Alvernia is the highest point in the Bahamas at 207 feet (63 m). At its peak stands the Hermitage, a medieval-style monastery built in 1939 by Father Jerome, a Roman Catholic priest who was also a skilled architect and sculptor.

Thunderball Grotto
Thunderball Grotto on Great Exuma Island was one of the sites used in the filming of two James Bond movies, *Thunderball* and *Never Say Never Again*. Visitors at low tide can enjoy the abundant marine life.

Dixon Hill Lighthouse
This lighthouse on San Salvador operates the old-fashioned way: It is fueled by kerosene that is pumped to the top to light the "mantle." Visitors can climb to the top of the 160-foot (49-m) structure, see the machinery, and get great views of the island.

ABOUT THE CULTURE

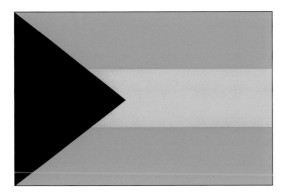

OFFICIAL NAME
Commonwealth of the Bahamas

LAND AREA
5,382 square miles (13,939 square km)

ESTIMATED TOTAL AREA
100,387 square miles (260,000 square km)

CAPITAL
Nassau (on New Providence)

MAJOR CITIES
Nassau, Freeport (on Grand Bahama)

ISLANDS
700 inhabited islands and cays, approximately 2,000 uninhabited islets. Principal islands: New Providence, Grand Bahama; Family Islands: the Abacos (Great Abaco, Little Abaco), Acklins, Andros, Berry Island, the Biminis, Cat Island, Crooked Island, Eleuthera, the Exumas, Harbour Island, the Inaguas (Little Inagua, Great Inagua), Long Island, Mayaguana, Ragged Island, San Salvador, Spanish Wells, and Walker's Cay

HIGHEST POINT
Mount Alvernia (207 feet/63 m)

POPULATION
309,156 (2009 estimate)

LIFE EXPECTANCY
total population: 65.78 years
male: 62.63 years
female: 68.98 years (2009 estimate)

BIRTHRATE
16.81 births/1,000 people (2009 estimate)

ETHNIC GROUPS
African-descent 85 percent, Caucasian 12 percent, Asian and Hispanic 3 percent

RELIGION
Baptist 35.4 percent, Anglican 15.1 percent, Roman Catholic 13.5 percent, Pentecostal 8.1 percent, Church of God 4.8 percent, Methodist 4.2 percent, other Christian 15.2 percent, none or unspecified 2.9 percent, others 0.8 percent

LANGUAGES
English (official), French Creole (among Haitian immigrants)

NATIONAL HOLIDAYS
New Year's Day, January 1; Good Friday, Friday before Easter; Easter Monday, Monday after Easter; Whit Monday, seven weeks after Easter; Labor Day, first Friday in June; Independence Day, July 10; Emancipation Day, first Monday in August; National Heroes' Day, October 12; Christmas Day, December 25; Boxing Day, December 26

TIME LINE

IN THE BAHAMAS	IN THE WORLD

6000 B.C.
Evidence for the use of chili peppers is found in the Bahamas.

A.D. 1492
Christopher Columbus makes his first landing in the New World, in the Bahamas.

1647
English and Bermudan religious refugees, the Eleutheran Adventurers, establish the first European settlement on the Bahamas.

1666
Colonization of New Providence Island begins.

1717
Bahamas becomes a British Crown colony.

1783
Spain cedes the Bahamas to Britain in accordance with the Treaty of Paris after briefly occupying the islands the previous year.

1834
Emancipation of slaves.

1940–45
The Duke of Windsor—formerly King Edward VIII—serves as governor of the Bahamas.

1950
Britain grants the United States a military test range and tracking station for guided missiles in the Bahamas.

1955
Free-trade area is established in the town of Freeport, stimulating tourism and attracting offshore banking.

1964
The Bahamas is granted internal autonomy.

1967
Lynden Pindling becomes prime minister after his centrist Progressive Liberal Party (PLP) wins the islands' first legislative elections.

1972
Negotiations with Britain over independence begin in the wake of an overwhelming victory in the elections by the PLP, which campaigns on a platform of independence.

1973
The Bahamas becomes independent.

---

753 B.C.
Rome is founded.

A.D. 1000
The Chinese perfect gunpowder and begin to use it in warfare.

1776
U.S. Declaration of Independence

1789–99
The French Revolution

1939
World War II begins.

IN THE BAHAMAS	IN THE WORLD

1983
Government ministers face allegations of drug trafficking.

1984
Pindling is endorsed as PLP leader after denying charges of corruption and ties to drug traffickers.

1986
Nuclear power disaster at Chernobyl in Ukraine

1991
Breakup of the Soviet Union

1992
Hubert Ingraham becomes prime minister after his center-left Free National Movement (FNM) wins a majority in the general elections, ending 25 years of rule by Pindling.

1996
Ingraham reinstates the death penalty for murder.

1997
Ingraham returns as prime minister after his party is reelected.

1997
Hong Kong is returned to China.

1998
Two convicted murderers are hanged despite international opposition and concern over the use of the death penalty in the Caribbean.

2000
"Father of independence" Sir Lynden Pindling dies in August. He was head of government from 1967 to 1992.

2001
Dame Ivy Dumont in November becomes the Bahamas's first woman governor-general.

2001
Terrorists crash planes into New York, Washington D.C., and Pennsylvania.

2002
Veteran politician Perry Christie leads the PLP to a landslide victory in May, unseating the FMN, which has been in power for 10 years.

2003
War in Iraq begins.

2004
Hurricane Frances sweeps through the Bahamas, causing widespread damage. Weeks later Hurricane Jeanne batters the Bahamas.

2006
UK-based court rules that the mandatory death sentence for murder breaches the Bahamian constitution. It was last used in 2000.

2007
Former prime minister Hubert Ingraham's FNM wins parliamentary elections in May.

2008
The first black president of the United States, Barack Obama, is elected.

GLOSSARY

atoll
A ring-shape coral reef or a string of closely spaced small coral islands, enclosing or nearly enclosing a shallow lagoon.

Baja Mar
Spanish for "shallow sea," which refers to the sea surrounding the Bahamian islands.

calipee
The part of a sea turtle next to the lower shield, consisting of a yellowish substance, considered a delicacy.

chatting
Call-and-answer musical improvisation or ad-libbing in Bahamian musical folktales and spirituals. Also known as "rigging."

conch
Mollusk popular in the Bahamas as a snack (such as fritters), a main dish, and an ingredient in a salad.

Eleutherian Adventurers
English Puritans who in the 17th century traveled to Eleuthera to start a settlement where they could worship according to their own rules.

Free National Movement (FNM)
Elected to power in 1992 and 1997, a political party formed in 1971 as a coalition of the United Bahamian Party and dissidents from the Progressive Liberal Party.

goombay
Music characterized by the rhythmic beat of goatskin drums accompanied by other instruments including whistles, click sticks, cowbells, bongos, maracas, and conch-shell horns.

grits
Coarsely ground cornmeal.

Junkanoo
Festival between Christmas and New Year, featuring elaborate costumed parades and goombay bands and dancers.

Kalik
A Bahamian beer.

***lukku-cairi* (LOOK-oo KAY-ri)**
"Island people," Lucayans' name for themselves.

obeah
Bahamian tradition of spirit healing based on superstition and African religious beliefs.

Progressive Liberal Party (PLP)
Political party founded in 1953.

rake 'n' scrape
Music made with instruments improvised from household implements and tools.

true-true Bahamian
A typical Bahamian, identifiable by speech idiosyncrasies and adherence to traditions.

FOR FURTHER INFORMATION

BOOKS

Barratt, Peter. *Bahama Saga: The Epic Story of the Bahama Islands.* Bloomington, IN: AuthorHouse, 2004.

Craton, Michale. *A—Z of Bahamas Heritage.* (Macmillan Caribbean A—Z). Oxford, England: Macmillan Caribbean, 2007.

Hassam, John Tyler. *The Bahama Islands: Notes on an Early Attempt at Colonization.* Charleston, SC: BiblioBazaar, 2008.

Hudgin, Thomas L. *Incident at Cat Island.* Bowling Green, KY: Hickory Tales Publishing, 2007.

Lester, George. *In Sunny Isles: Chapters Treating Chiefly of the Bahamas Islands and Cuba.* Charleston, SC: BiblioBazaar, 2008.

Lewis, Sara et al. *Explorer Chartbook Near Bahamas.* 3rd ed. Ocean City, MD: Lewis Offshore, 2004.

Maples, Don. *The Making of the Bahamas.* 2nd ed. London: Longman, 2004.

Smith, Larry. *The Bahamas: Portrait of an Archipelago.* Oxford, England: Macmillan Caribbean, 2004.

Williams, Colleen and Madonna Flood. *Bahamas* (The Caribbean Today). Broomall, PA: Mason Crest Publishers, 2009.

WEBSITES

Bahamas Online. www.thebahamas.com/

CIA—The World Factbook: the Bahamas. www.cia.gov/library/publications/the-world-factbook/geos/bf.html

The Islands of the Bahamas. www.bahamas.com

Lonely Planet—the Bahamas. www.lonelyplanet.com/the-bahamas

FILM

The Best Bahamas Beaches Dive Travel—Grand Bahama Island with Gary Knapp. GRK Productions Inc., 2009.

MUSIC

Bahama Llama. *Baja Whale Watching.* Phantom Sound & Vision, 2008.

Various artists. *Cult Cargo: Grand Bahama Goombay.* Numero, 2007.

Various artists. *Kneeling Down Inside the Gate: The Great Rhyming Singers of the Bahamas.* Rounder, 2009.

BIBLIOGRAPHY

BOOKS

Carillet, Jean-Bernard and Jill Kirby. *Lonely Planet Bahamas, Turks & Caicos.* 3rd ed. Victoria, Australia: Lonely Planet Publications, 2005.

Charles, Ron. *Bahamas Guide.* 4th ed. Cold Spring Harbor, NY: Open Road, 2004.

Folster, Natalie and Gaylord Dold. *The Rough Guide to the Bahamas.* 2nd ed. London: Rough Guide Travel Guides, 2007.

Howard, Blair and Renate Siekmann. *Adventure Guide to the Bahamas, Turks and Caicos.* Walpole, MA: Hunter Publishing, 2007.

McCulla, Patricia E. *Bahamas* (Major World Nations Series). Broomall, PA: Chelsea House, 1998.

Neely, Wayne. *Recollections of Some of the Greatest Storms to Affect the Bahamas.* Bloomington, IN: AuthorHouse, 2006.

Porter, Darwin and Danforth Prince. *Frommer's Bahamas 2010.* Hoboken, NJ: Wiley Publishing, 2009.

WEBSITES

The Bahamas Meteorology Department. www.bahamasweather.org.bs/.

The Bahamian: Cultural History, Activities, and Festivals. www.cultural.thebahamian.com.

The Central Bank of the Bahamas. www.centralbankbahamas.com/.

CIA—The World Factbook: the Bahamas. www.cia.gov/library/publications/the-world-factbook/geos/bf.html.

The Commonwealth of the Bahamas. www.bahamas.gov.bs.

FoodReference.com: Bahamas Food Festivals. www.foodreference.com/html/bahamas-food-festivals.html.

Geographia: Bahamas—Acklins and Crooked Island. www.geographia.com/bahamas/.

Governments on the WWW: Bahamas. www.gksoft.com/govt/en/bs.html.

HotelTravel.com: Bahamas. www.hoteltravel.com/bahamas/guides/festivals.htm.

The Islands of the Bahamas. www.bahamas.com.

Lonely Planet—the Bahamas. www.lonelyplanet.com/the-bahamas.

The Permanent Mission of the Commonwealth of the Bahamas to the United Nations. www.un.int/bahamas/Bahamas_Government_Info.htm.

Political Resources. www.politicalresources.net/bahamas.htm.

QandA.com. www.qanda.encyclopedia.com/question/type-government-does-bahamas-have-80700.html.

INDEX

INDEX